28 New Age Healing Therapies

28 New Age Healing Therapies

Luis S.R. Vas

Publishers
Pustak Mahal®

J-3/16 , Daryaganj, New Delhi-110002
☎ 23276539, 23272783, 23272784 • *Fax:* 011-23260518
E-mail: info@pustakmahal.com • *Website:* www.pustakmahal.com

Sales Centre

- 10-B, Netaji Subhash Marg, Daryaganj, New Delhi-110002
  ☎ 23268292, 23268293, 23279900 • *Fax:* 011-23280567
  E-mail: rapidexdelhi@indiatimes.com
- **Hind Pustak Bhawan**
  6686, Khari Baoli, Delhi-110006
  ☎ 23944314, 23911979

Branches

Bengaluru: ☎ 080-22234025 • *Telefax:* 080-22240209
E-mail: pustak@airtelmail.in • pustak@sancharnet.in
Mumbai: ☎ 022-22010941, 022-22053387
E-mail: rapidex@bom5.vsnl.net.in
Patna: ☎ 0612-3294193 • *Telefax:* 0612-2302719
E-mail: rapidexptn@rediffmail.com
Hyderabad: *Telefax:* 040-24737290
E-mail: pustakmahalhyd@yahoo.co.in

This book was earlier published under the title
"Master Approaches to New Age Alternative Therapies"

ISBN 978-81-223-0745-0

Edition: 2011

Printed at : **Unique Colour Cartoon, Delhi**

CONTENTS

INTRODUCTION

Alternative medicine has enjoyed increasing popularity in recent years. This success has been largely due to the failure of traditional medicine in handling chronic ailments as well as due to its high costs. This has led numerous medical practitioners, including allopathic doctors, to try their hand at complementary and drugless medicines, incorporating insights from wisdom traditions of the world.

In this book we bring together the approaches of some notable practitioners both ancient and modern, who have enjoyed remarkable success with their patients and have developed a wide following. Their philosophies, their practical approaches and the outcome of their researches are presented to the reader in a spirit of sharing in the hope that a wider audience will benefit from their innovations.

We do not prescribe any of these approaches. The reader is advised to check with his or her own physician before following any of the prescriptions offered here.

—Luis S.R. Vas

1

ANCIENT MASTERS

HEALING THROUGH MANTRAS AND YANTRAS

Mantra meditation is often called "Mantra Yoga", considered to be a part of "Nada Yoga", which means the "yoga of sound". The word "yoga" means to "link with God" and this is the ultimate goal of all yoga. Today many people know nothing of yoga. Although used as a means to keeping good physical condition, in reality this is but a by-product of yoga. The physical postures or "asanas" are to help bring the senses under control in order to prepare for meditation . Control over the urges of the external senses (tongue, belly, and genitals) is required to actually engage in true meditation. Ultimately the mind will be also brought under control. Yoga is the science of self-realisation as enunciated in the Vedas, India's ancient holy scriptures, which are told to be descended from God Himself, not from man's comprehension and expositions of relative truths. Therefore Veda means "truth", and the truths contained are as universal and equally applicable today just as they were many thousands of years ago.

In the Vedas there are said to be four ages or "yugas" in each dawning of new creation, made up of a total of some millions of years. In each yuga there was a recommended system of yoga in accordance with the mentality and ability of the populace during the time. At this time we are in the early stages of the "Kali-Yuga' (5,000 years have passed and 427,000 years remain), also known as the "age of quarrel and hypocrisy", a time when both our lives and memories are extremely short. Therefore in this age it is not possible for us to engage in the mystic yoga system. To practise this system there must be complete control of all senses, going into yogic trance as a prelude to self-realisation. (Of course, it's necessary to spend some thousands of years doing so to achieve the goal by undergoing this difficult process!).

Therefore in this age it is not possible to achieve it in this way as, not only do we live even less than 100 years, but who among us can concentrate with such intensity in silence, oblivious to all bodily urges or conveniences? Accordingly in this period mantra yoga, or mantra meditation, is the only viable means for self-realisation. There are many scriptural injunctions confirming that the "holy names of God" are the only means of crossing the ocean of maya (illusion) in order to become realised and thus free from the bonds of material life. The old rishis, seers or saints of ancient India passed down these sacred sound vibrations for the benefit of all life but especially for human society for only in the human form of life can one obtain spiritual realisation. Although animals benefit from hearing transcendental sound vibrations, they cannot achieve spiritual self-realisation unless or until they are prompted to the human form of life. These sacred sound vibrations are known to promote healing on all levels, whilst, at the same time, awakening the chakras within our ethereal, or subtle, bodies. Mantras are always sung to a melody (raga), although it is generally monophonic, or individual, sounds which may 'seem' to be without harmony. The Greeks, as did other cultures, understood music to be mathematical and, as Pythagoras taught, they made the equally interesting connection between sound, music and the science of astronomy. In " Poetica" Aristotle stated that poetry comprised language, rhythm and sound. He also pointed towards the potency of sound vibrations to influence human thoughts and emotions.

The Meaning of Mantra

Mantras, being sacred sound vibrations, are composed of sacred syllables representative of and containing within great spiritual power, or energy. Utilising mantras allows us to concentrate and focus this spiritual energy. The mantras were perceived originally by the great seers or rishis from the primaeval or cosmic ether and translated into very definite syllables with rhythm and melody.

The word "mantra" is composed, in sanskrit, of two root words. " Man" means "mind", or "thinking", and "tra" to "release or free". Therefore the meaning is to free the mind and thinking from the material sphere of consciousness and to be able to transcend the wheel of "samsara" or "birth and death within this physical world".

Chanting mantra promotes harmony on all levels as it awakens the spiritual self. Once awakened, ultimately the spiritual self or soul, turns within to the source of all power and can direct spiritual energy not only for personal benefit but for the good of all others. All mantras have six aspects, a seer or rishi, a raga, a presiding deity (Devata), a seed sound (bija), power (shakti) and pillar (kilaka).

Rishis' Mantras have always come down from master to disciple, beginning with the ancient seers, or rishis. It is said that unless a mantra is received from an authorised source it will be ineffectual. Therefore this process has been kept intact since time immemorial. Just as different tones cause specific vibrations which have an effect on the physical and emotional self, practising mantra meditation correctly will allow the sound vibration to be connected with specific images and to understand that the sound vibration is contained within these images.

Devata Sound vibrations represent very definitive forms and repeated chanting of a mantra will gradually reveal the form of the deity, or devata, central to the mantra. This worship of the form then becomes the centre of the aspirant's consciousness. This allows the aspirant to develop a personal relationship with the presiding deity of the mantra. There are many mantras for different results but the ultimate are the mantras for realising our relationship with the Supreme Lord. There are many levels of consciousness, as well as desire, among human beings and many mantras for achieving various goals. We will speak about the numerous types of mantras further on in this chapter but, suffice it to say, that the most important mantras are those which invoke the practitioner to bring about a desire for spiritual service, culminating in absolute love. At this point the aspirant may achieve the perfection of desire....to desire only that which is transcendental to this world of birth, death, old-age and disease.

Bija within each mantra is its seed (bija) which is its source of potency. Just as it is impossible to see the tree within the seed, yet it is there waiting for fructification, it is also not possible to see the spiritual self within until it is time. However, through regular discipline of chanting mantra the true "self" will eventually be realised. How quickly depends on the sincerity and desires of the aspirant. There are some mantras utilised simply for temporary gain within this material world and although we will give some descriptions of these, this is not the goal of chanting mantra. Only spiritual self-realisation is the ultimate goal. All other desires are stumbling blocks on the path to self realisation.

Pillar (kilaka) is the will-power that an aspirant must gain to regularly practice the mantra until it becomes automatic.

Shakti is the power held within the mantra. Ultimately a taste develops most especially in chanting mantras glorifying and extolling the qualities of God. We all have an"original" consciousness. The goal of life is to understand who we are, where we have come from and what is our purpose. Chanting mantras for any other purpose will not bear permanent fruit. Those utilised for any other purposes of a temporary nature must be chanted with perfect rhythm, tone and harmony and neither the raga, nor key, may be changed to any variation whatsoever. In today's world how many can develop such concentration and expertise over such a short life span?...Not very many. Fortunately, God is merciful and to indulge in the chanting of any ONE of the unlimited names of the Supreme Godhead as a devout mantra, even if imperfect, will have an effect. The only prerequisite is that the mantra is received from one who can properly impart it and train the aspirant in the basis of developing spiritual life and the resultant spiritual consciousness.

Yantras

Often the subject of "yantra" evokes stares of incomprehension. If you then say "sacred geometry" some will understand, as this is what the modem scholars of ancient Egypt refer to their ancient system of yantra as. Many will also understand if you mention "mandala" as the Tibetan forms of mandala are more well known in the west. The particular shapes and figures have often been picked up and used commercially as poster prints which people place on their walls for decoration, not having the slightest idea of the intent of such a diagram Many ancient Vedic yantras, which are the oldest known, such as the concentric expanding diagram of "Sri Yantra" are mistakenly referred to as "mandalas" by the so-called "new-age" community.

All ancient cultures had sacred geometric designs representative of their Gods, which had a mantra (or sacred sound vibration) that corresponded to it. Indians, Egyptians, Jews, Chinese, and Mayans all had systems of "planetary yantras" used to combat malefic influences. Yantra is the ultimate "symbology". In the Vedic culture we find much power and energy said to be held within sacred geometric symbols. They are to be found throughout sacred scriptures, carved in stone, hidden within paintings and in temples.

One example of how a western "madman" tried to use these powers for personal gain (of an evil disposition) is the case of Adolph Hitler. The swastika is actually an ancient, holy symbol found in temples all over the east. It is especially seen in paintings and carved into the temples and thrones for deities of Lord Ganesh (the elephant-headed god of prosperity said to remove impediments and obstacles from the path of human endeavour) . Hitler actually drew the symbol improperly and, although it looks like the original to the untrained eye at a glance, it is wrong and had no potency. Furthermore there is much more to yielding the power behind yantra than simply having the diagram.

There is the dedication and effort required to yield the beneficial effects of chanting mantras, especially if they are for some material purpose. Yantras are not "lucky charms" to be worn or displayed as icons of power in and of themselves. Much specific knowledge and ability must go into their preparation and much dedication is required to achieve the desired effects. Yantra means a "mystical diagram", "talisman", or "instrument" which, if prepared and created by a qualified "Tantric" (one qualified in the knowledge and practice of Tantra) as well as utilised under their specific instructions for fruitful results, will help to gain the objector objects of desire or ambition. Yantras are used in worship (puja) and can also be an effective instrument used towards the aim of self-realisation. The Vedic scriptures speak of them as worshipable and they were used by the ancient saints, seers, and rishis.

Yantras and mantras are connected together as for each yantra (diagram) there is a corresponding mantra that must be used with it they are representative of different deities from different demigods all the way up to the Supreme Personality of Godhead. There is also a definite relationship between them and the material elements of earth, water, fire, air and ether. By proper prayers, worship, and perfect recitation of specific mantras the material elements, or material nature, may be induced to move in a way the practitioner desires. This is not magic, nor trickery, but a highly evolved and developed science for exercising some control in this regard.

A zero ("nought" to the British or 'bindu" in Sanskrit) is the basis of the geometry through which the yantric triangle is developed. It is said to represent the different desires within the heart, the ways of fulfilling them and the acquisition of knowledge.

This "bindu" is the central point. By concentrating on the bindu the ability to concentrate and build up a powerful mental or psychic force field is increased. It is broadened and, in its expansion, many other kinds of shapes are formed. These figures or geometric shapes are what are termed the "yantra" Although it would not be a difficult task for most of us to copy the form of a yantra, it would not have the desired effect. Furthermore to be perfectly honest, it would be all but useless if not created by a qualified person ('Tantric") and then "infused" with the specific energy via the medium of mantra. Otherwise it becomes just an interesting form or picture to look at, but has no real effect on time or circumstances within life.

The physical manifestation of the yantra itself is generally drawn or etched into metal, be it gold, silver, bronze, copper, lead, or stainless steel, although paper is sometimes used for their inscription.

Such materials are long lasting with the idea that when the worship, or puja, is performed, the person the yantra is meant for will have protection from evil and undesirable forces of nature. To constantly increase its effectiveness the user must perform certain worship and regularly chant the prescribed mantras.

Mantras and yantras must be used with the utmost care, dedication and spiritual energy through regular chanting to be effective. Due to the highly advanced and evolved souls necessary to create dedicate, install and worship the yantra initially, they may seem to be ineffective in this day and age. However, it's not due to any defects within the revealed knowledge and science of yantra, but to the lack of dedication and ability of most to achieve the results. These sacred diagrams of "yantra" are representative of time and space and can most especially be seen within the most sacred and powerful yantra, the "Sri Yantra" . There are 90 many very exacting levels to be gone through in their preparation and specific rituals that absolutely must be performed perfectly during this step-by-step procedure, that their creation is extremely difficult and specialised.

There is an irrevocable connection between the yogic and tantric (which contains the science of yantra) paths and between the process of worship and attainment Initially, in a tantric's practice, specific ceremony is effected absolutely linked to the astronomical sciences.

The tantric then creates a visualisation of being "central" or located in the inner middle of the spinal column, the centre of which is called "Meru". This is also called the "sushumna", through which the "kundalini" (coiled up energy or "shakti" within the chakra at the base of the spine) passes .

This is the whole aim or ambition of the tantric, that his "kundalini" will ascend the "sushumna" and remain concentrated in the chakra between the eyebrows until the correct auspicious moment. At this time, success may be achieved by raising the kundalini to the crown chakra and ultimately brought forth to a destination beyond this world, leaving the material body in the flames of yogic fire.

Types of Yantras

Bhu Prisht Yantras: Bhu means Earth and Bhu Devi is the name of Mother Earth. Accordingly they are made from materials found within the earth, as the name implies. There are two subdivisions. The first is raised yantras which include the bija mantras and vern mantras. The second is carved yantras.

Meru Prisht Yantras: Raised, with a wide base, thinner midsection and peaked top in the shape of a mountain.

Patel Yantras: Carved, in the shape of an inverted mountain, making it the opposite of the Meru Prisht yantra.

Meru Parastar Yantras: These are of the Meru, mountain shape, but cut, rather than raised.

Ruram Prisht Yantras: Have tortoise shell tops on a rectangular base.

These five types of yantras are classed according to the different puja (worship) conducted. Each has a separate and distinct purpose to gain a particular objective for the aspirant. Some yantras are worshipped in temples, some worshipped by individuals at home and some are worn on the body (usually of triangular or rectangular shape) either around the neck, the arms, or kept close to the body in another location. According to how the yantras are used they are further classified into seven divisions, as follows:

Sharir Yantras: There are seven of these yantras, one for each of the "chakras" . They are worn on the body and each has its own mantras. Chanting these mantras bestows various benefits to the aspirant.

Dharan Yantras: These yantras are also worn on the body and include particular ritual s producing different results .

Asana Yantras: These yantras are positioned under the asana (sitting place) during puja. They are said to bear their fruit more quickly than other yantras and therefore are generally placed under the foundations of homes and temple s sometimes even under the worshipped deity of the home or temple, to bring the favourable results in a fairly short span of time.

Mandala Yantras: These yantras are created using nine people to participate in the puja. They arrange their sitting places in the form of the yantra. One participant sits in the centre, another to the north, north-east, east, south-east, south, south west, west and one north-west. The aspirant in the centre position offers the puja of the " Ishat" mantra and the eight others also chant individual specific mantras at the same time.

Puja Yantras: These yantras are installed, whether in temples or individuals' homes, while puja is taking place. There are different yantras to serve various desires. They may be for different religious deity worship, or for the different planets in our solar system. The worship and installation of these yantras is of five basic steps:

1. Before the performance of the puja, the yantras are installed as icons, or worshipable deities. The yantras are drawn numerically and while offering the puja, the names of the respective "devas" (according to the numbers) are chanted throughout the mantras.
2. In the centre of the yantra is written the name of the particular deva being worshipped, then the puja is performed.
3. Either the first word of the mantra, the bija mantra, or the full mantra is written whilst preparing the yantra itself.
4. A carving, painting, or photograph of the deva and worshipable deity is attached to the yantra before beginning the puja.
5. Full-colour pictures of deva or worshipable deity are applied to the yantra.

Chatar Yantras: These yantras are not placed upon the body, but kept in the pocket, or under a turban (or hat)

Darshan Yantras: These yantras are generally found in temples. 'Darshan' means to take advantage of the association with a deity or other representative form of God, or His devotee. It is said that if an aspirant sees them during the morning hours, they will be benefic in awarding success. These are greatly "purified' yantras and are installed in great historic temples.

■ ■ ■

2

ANDREW WEIL

HEALING THROUGH BETTER EATING AND BREATHING

Dr. Andrew Weil may be among the world's leading experts on nutrition. He believes that eating should be an enjoyable, social activity. The bestselling author of Eight Weeks to Optimum Health and Eating Well for Optimum Health: The Essential Guide to Food, Diet and Nutrition, Weil has traveled the world, studying the diets of many different cultures to see how they make their cuisine both healthy and fun.

In Eating Well for Optimum Health he recommends different diets for improving and maintaining health. He feels that most conventional doctors are hesitant to prescribe therapeutic diets because they are constrained by their ignorance. Nutrition still is not being taught in medical schools, so doctors have to educate themselves.

The profession is still dominated by an old guard that provides obsolete nutritional advice. They are also heavily influenced by the food industries — the meat and dairy industries, for instance. But it is changing. Dr. Weil hopes that soon registered dieticians can become a powerful force for disseminating the right kind of nutritional information.

He emphasizes that learning to read food labels is important. If the label barely has space to list all the ingredients, put it back on the shelf. If you see words like "partially hydrogenated oils" of any kind, put it back. If it has artificial colours or sweeteners or is high in sodium, put it back. Then look at the fat content and the kind of fat or oil in it. Look at the total carbohydrate content as well as the kinds of carbohydrates. In his book Eating Well for Optimum Health, he has a chapter on reading labels, with examples from actual food products.

Partially hydrogenated oils are unnatural, artificially treated fats that he thinks promote cancer, heart disease, and degenerative changes in cells. There is no reason for them to be in food, other than that they are convenient for manufacturers. If there is enough consumer awareness about them, then we can get them out of foods just like we eliminated highly saturated palm and coconut oils, he says. The irony is that those tropical oils are probably less dangerous than the partially hydrogenated fats that have replaced them.

Glucose is the simplest fuel, the basic energy currency of all cells in the body, he says. Most foods are converted to glucose, transported around the blood, and burned in that form. The brain, for instance, can run only on glucose and needs a constant, unvarying supply.

We can keep glucose levels in balance by eating a balanced diet that is a proper mix of carbohydrates, fats, and proteins. It's easiest for the body to obtain glucose from carbohydrates, then from fat, then from protein. We are in a period where people are demonizing carbohydrates, he says, but in fact, you need carbohydrates in the right form to maintain glucose levels and feed the brain.

One of the most surprising facts on a Weil video is that, idlis, a highly touted health food, is not good for you. One thing that the anti-carbohydrate diet-book authors are saying is true: All carbohydrates are not created equal.

Carbohydrates are rated on what is called the glycemic index, which shows the rate at which carbohydrates convert to glucose. The more we refine carbohydrates, puff them up, and mill them into fine powders, the larger the starch's surface area and the faster they turn to glucose. For those who are "carbohydrate sensitive" (about a third of us), this is probably the most important thing driving weight gain. Idlis, which many consider an austere diet food, actually have a high glycemic index because the exploded rice grains are easily converted to blood sugar.

Sensitiveness to carbohydrates it is not an allergy, but probably an inherited trait, which was a selective advantage in the old days before carbohydrates were widely available. People who have this genetic trait can easily take advantage of carbohydrate's caloric energy when it is readily available. But those who have this genetic trait now — in a world so full of sugar and refined starches — tend to gain weight easily, especially in the abdomen. Blood pressure tends to be high, and they become resistant to the effects of insulin, which in its extreme form, leads to adult-onset diabetes.

How does a person determine whether or not they are carbohydrate sensitive? Weil answers: look at your family history. Is there a history of coronary heart disease, adult-onset diabetes, and hypertension? Do you tend to gain weight easily and have a tendency toward high blood pressure and high serum triglycerides (blood fats)?

Many people enjoy eating huge portions of meat and have never really liked vegetables. Now there's a diet telling them they can eat all the meat they want. You can lose weight on this crash diet, but it is not good over the long-term. When you eat too much protein, you put a big workload on the liver and kidneys and probably irritate the immune system. And you are not giving the brain its preferred fuel source, according to Weil.

Weil thinks the Mediterranean diet looks the healthiest, is the most adaptable. It is a composite of the ways people eat in Spain, France, Italy, Greece, Crete, and the Middle East. The diet is relatively low in animal foods — low in red meat and poultry — but higher in fish. It includes some dairy in the form of cheese and yogurt, but not much sugar. Mediterranean people eat plenty of fruits and vegetables and grainy carbohydrates like pasta cooked al dente and chewy breads. And they use enough olive oil to make life interesting. It's a diet with taste appeal, and populations who eat this way have a low rate of cancer and heart disease.

It's good to have a mix of raw and cooked vegetables. "I don't think an all-raw diet is good. Many vegetables contain toxins that are easily destroyed by cooking. And some nutrients become more available to the body in cooked form, like the carotene pigments of carrots and dark leafy greens. These pigments are oil soluble, meaning they need fats to get transported across the walls of the gut."

If you are carbohydrate sensitive, to lose weight the most important thing is to moderate consumption of the high glycemic index carbohydrate foods. Eat less refined starches and sugars. For everybody, though, the main thing is to decrease the calories you eat and to increase activity. Eat less. Exercise more.

Either people are scared into a healthier lifestyle by a disease scare — like chest pain or a lump in their breast — or people are motivated by something that makes them conscious of their body image. A better sort of motivation is realizing, through education, that certain eating habits are better for long-term health. But people need to understand that these changes in diet can be made gradually. Improve in small increments to give yourself time to adjust.

Relaxation breathing strongly influences mind, body, and moods, says Weil. By simply putting your attention on your breathing, without even doing anything to change it, you move in the direction of relaxation. There are many worse places to have your attention: on your thoughts, for one, since thoughts are the source of much of our anxiety, guilt, and unhappiness. Get in the habit of shifting your awareness to your breath whenever you find yourself dwelling on upsetting thoughts. The single most effective relaxation technique I know, says Weil, is conscious regulation of breath. Here is a yogic breathing exercise Weil gives to most of his patients. It is utterly simple, takes almost no time, requires no equipment, and can be done anywhere.

Although you can do the exercise in any position, to learn it he suggests you do it seated with your back straight. Place the tip of your tongue against the ridge of tissue just behind your upper front teeth, and keep it there through the entire exercise. You will be exhaling through your mouth around your tongue; try pursing your lips slightly if this seems awkward.

First exhale completely through your mouth, making a whoosh sound. Next close your mouth and inhale quietly through your nose to a mental count of four. Next hold your breath for a count of seven. Then exhale completely through your mouth, making a whoosh sound to a count of eight.

This is one breath. Now inhale again and repeat the cycle three more times for a total of four breaths. Note that you always inhale quietly through your nose and exhale audibly through your mouth. The tip of your tongue stays in position the whole time. Exhalation takes twice as long as inhalation. The absolute time you spend on each phase is not important; the ratio of 4:7:8 is important. If you have trouble holding your breath, speed the exercise up but keep to the ratio of 4:7:8 for the three phases.

With practice you can slow it all down and get used to inhaling and exhaling more and more deeply. This exercise is a natural tranquilizer for the nervous system.

Unlike tranquilizing drugs, which are often effective when you first take them but lose their power over time, this exercise is subtle when you first try it but gains in power with repetition and practice. Weil recommends you to do it at least twice a day. You cannot do it too frequently. Do not do more than four breaths at one time for the first month of practice. Later, if you wish, you can extend it to eight breaths. If you feel a little lightheaded when you first breathe this way, do not be concerned; it will pass.

You may also notice an immediate shift in consciousness after four of these breaths, a feeling of detachment or lightness or dreaminess, for example. That shift is desirable and will increase with repetition. It is a sign that you are affecting your involuntary nervous system and neutralizing stress. Once you develop this technique by practising it every day, it will be a very useful tool that you will always have with you. Use it whenever anything upsetting happens, before you react, he advises. Use it whenever you are aware of internal tension. Use it to help you fall asleep. He says he cannot recommend this exercise too highly. Everyone can benefit from it.

People often ask Weil the reason for keeping the tongue in that position. Yoga philosophy describes two "nerve currents" in the human body, one positive, electric, and solar, the other negative, magnetic, and lunar. These begin and end at the tip of the tongue and the ridge behind the upper front teeth. Putting those structures in contact is supposed to complete a circuit, keeping the energy of the breath within instead of letting it dissipate. "I don't know if there is any correlation between these ideas and Western concepts of physiology, but since yogis have been doing this exercise for thousands of years, it seems worth following their instructions exactly," he says.

■ ■ ■

3

BARBARA BRENNAN

HEALING THROUGH THE AURA

Science and spirituality are often at loggerheads with each other, and few can be considered experts in both fields. Barbara Brennan SM is a former NASA physicist, holding a graduate degree in Atmospheric Physics, and worked as a research scientist at NASA's Goddard Space Flight Centre in Maryland. But she is also a holistic healer: a graduate of New York's Institute of Core Energetics and a Senior Pathwork Helper for those following that holistic health path.

Brennan has spent over two decades researching and exploring the human energy field. Her first book, Hands of Light: A Guide to Healing Through the Human Energy Field won widespread renown. It has appeared in 15 languages and more than three million copies are in print worldwide, testifying to her growing popularity.

In the late 1990s she founded the Barbara Brennan School of Healing® in East Hampton, New York, which offered a four-year Professional Healing Science certification course. She is director of the school where the present enrolment exceeds 700 students, and continues to conduct workshops on Healing Science throughout the world.

She claims that the healing techniques she teaches are based on the anatomy and physiology of the human energy field or auric field. She teaches people how to perceive and "read" the human energy field. With the auric field, she says, you can perceive how every decision and everything you experience in your life affects your body. It all shows in the auric field, every thought, every feeling and every sensation. The auric field has a specific pattern of health, according to Brennan. The way we deal with our life experiences, or how we react to negative experiences in our lives, are reflected in the aura. When we distort our energy fields, she says, that has a direct and immediate

effect on the physical body. It might be slight at first, but if we habitually react to situations in a negative way, the habitual reaction will eventually show in the physical body and cause a physical disturbance.

A trained healer, according to Brennan, works with a client's energy field to clear it of unhealthy or blocked energies, charge depleted areas, repair distorted patterns and balance the entire auric field. This energy work promotes health and healing on the physical, emotional, mental and spiritual levels.

"I'm most excited about what I've been channeling for my students and how that is leading us into what I refer to as the ascension process," Brennan observes. "I personally channel a lecture for each of the four years of training, during each class meeting. These lectures are spiritual guidance for all members of the school. The origin and development of the Barbara Brennan School of Healing® (BBSH) over the 14 years of its existence has been informed by the information received through these channelings."

The healing process includes 'ascension' which means to move from a physically-based reality to a consciousness-and then spiritually-based reality. It is only through the ascension process that we will be able to solve the many problems faced by humanity today, she believes. It seems to her that we are moving into the ascension process as we move into the 21st century. When we cannot blame our irrational behavior on someone or something, we become consciously aware of how utterly preposterous it is! It can be seen as just a bad habit that we need to let go of. Of course, she maintains, this takes a lot of courage because it means letting go of our self-identity as we know it. It doesn't mean letting go of individuality but, she emphasizes, as things change so drastically, one's "little ego" certainly doesn't think so. This is the preliminary step into the process of ascension.

As we are guided through the ascension experience, we are also changing our view of the space-time continuum. Channeling has always stated that time is a commodity of limitation that we hold ourselves locked into. It can be a tool of creation, but first, we must change our limited concepts of it to enable us to move through different types of "time." The trouble, she says, is that we link time to our mental constructs of physical reality.

"My channeling process has taught us that time is created from within each of us," says Brennan. When we breathe in, we move forward into the future. When we breathe out, we can move into the past. When we pause, we move into the experience of the now, the moment that includes all time. Perhaps "spherical time", she suggests, is a good term. Thus, rather than linking time to our mental constructs of physical reality, we can link time to the life pulse that arises from within us.

Brennan claims that when we surrender to the experience of time being linked to our life pulse as it moves through our energy bodies, our entire life experience is transformed and we descend into a deep experience of the divinity within each cell of our bodies. It is a deeply moving, highly pleasurable state of being connected to all that there is. There is no division between anything, and yet there is the experience of individuality. "In the last channeling I did," she says, "I had the experience of being the Holy Galactic Body of the Milky Way. That is, I consciously became the galaxy. Many others in the room of some 750 people experienced the same thing. What was amazing for me about this experience was that it was so deeply physical. I didn't expect that. I thought ascension was about leaving the earth for higher spiritual realities, but this experience included all of it. What was necessary to get to such a place was to let go of the preconceived ideas about physical reality by which we live."

Sacred ceremonies are part of Barbara Brennan's programme. She believes that the sacred ceremonies put the creative process into action. They were created through the collaboration of the elders in the school and the school of shamans, and have emerged as multicultural healing journeys. "We believe," she says, "that these ceremonies are an opportunity to bring forth the Energetic Healing paradigm into life-transforming experiences, that this work is coming from the merging of sacred energies, that these experiences are unique to ourselves and the cultures we come form, and that they are part of the evolution of global consciousness. The ceremony themes for this year include Spiral Dance, Death, Spirit Canoe and the Journey to Shambala. Spiral Dance deals with the sacred metrical form of the spiral and helps students give away obstructions to their growth. Students create a huge number of spirals on the floor and enter into a spiral dance of initiation. An elder in the center is the gateway to the other world. The Death Ceremony is about going within and allowing that which needs to die to do so, thus allowing the soul's creative expression to emerge. The ceremony involves rattling, drumming and singing."

When Brennan was a NASA physicist, she found that the work she was doing — research with weather satellites — was exciting, but that still she felt there was something missing for her personally. She lived in Washington, D.C. in the early 70's when there was a lot of radical unrest going on. She got involved in the humanistic movement and began developing this other side of herself. She got much more interested in internal space than outer space, she discloses.

About a year or so after she resigned from NASA, she read books on meditation and got involved in training. It was then that she began seeing auras again, as she had when she was a child. She applied what she had learned from working with light-sensitive devices for satellites to how she was perceiving the aura. She utilized the basic knowledge of physics when working with infrared or ultraviolet light, and applied it to working with auras. "This worked very well because what came out of that was the ability to perceive different levels of the auric field. I could then teach people how to do that so that we could see more specifically what was going on in the auric field. From my perspective, it was repeatable. The thing about science is that something is considered real if it is repeatable. I have been able to teach hundreds of people to perceive the same things over and over again."

■ ■ ■

4

BARBARA HUBBARD

HEALING THROUGH CONSCIOUS EVOLUTION

Barbara Marx Hubbard, Educator, Futurist, best-selling author of Conscious Evolution, public speaker and president of the Foundation for Conscious Evolution. In the 1980s she presented a 14-part television series, Potentials, interviewing some of our greatest futurists, including Buckminster Fuller, Norman Cousins, Gene Roddenberry and Willis Harman. She lived in Marin County for many years, and currently resides in Santa Barbara, California.

The Foundation for Conscious Evolution has as its purpose to bring a new world view, called 'Conscious Evolution,' into the global culture. It is based on the belief that humankind holds within it the most hopeful guidelines for a positive future of any world view now available. By Conscious Evolution is meant that humans have gained the power of co-destruction and co-creation. By learning that we are actually responsible in some growing way for guiding the evolutionary process on this planet, means we have to learn a whole new set of skills, spiritually, socially and technologically. So the Foundation bringing the new world view of Conscious Evolution into the global culture. The work they are doing in Santa Barbara, is very exciting and new. It started in October 1998, when Hubbard was doing a speech in Santa Barbara. After she did her talk on Conscious Evolution, she asked a question: "What would happen if this community were to experience its own potential for Conscious Evolution?" She had never asked that question before. She said, "Would anybody here be interested?" And about 180 people put their names in a box. So then a group formed to bring her to Santa Barbara to do some kind of introductory teaching, which she did. And she said, "There are some things I think we need to know, to realize our full potential. First, we need to know our new story of creation, which is "cosmogenesis." The universe is, has been, is now evolving through us. And in that process of evolution, it has led to higher consciousness and greater freedom through more complex order. So we're placing ourselves as humans in the process of cosmogenesis. Also, we need to know that we–wherever we are in our personal lives, whether we're depressed or full of motivation–that the universe is in us, moving us. And it's my theory that there's a whole crop of people evolving into what might be called a 'universal human'."

Cultural Creatives, according to Hubbard, are people changing their values towards a more planetary and global culture. But over and above them she sees something deeper. She believes that there's an emerging species in humanity that has been pre-figured by the great avatars, Jesus, Buddha, and others. But that is becoming a new norm, as we expand in consciousness, expand in empathy, expand in connectedness, expand in creativity. she believes that we are, in a way, a transitional species, between the self-conscious homo sapiens, and what might eventually become a truly universal species, spiritually and physically. Because we are going to be moving outward; we are already working and living in space. By the third millennium, we will be a solar system species, if we don't blow ourselves up. By the fourth millennium, we may well be galactic.

The Cultural Creatives are a step along the way. But there's something of a deeper nature happening among the Cultural Creatives, and others, which she calls "Emergence." She says it feels almost like a shift of identity, from the separated self-centered stage to a more unified stage. And in that shift of identity, there's a maturation of our consciousness, and our creative responsibility, that I think is the harbinger of what we may be 2,000 from now. We have had homo habilus, homo erectus, homo neanderthal, homo sapiens…we are becoming homo universalis, a universal humanity. If you add the capacity for unitive consciousness for self-healing, and even eventually regeneration, and the capacity for the information revolution, and the global brain, and the capacity to live and work in space, and so on, you begin to see radical new powers, spiritually, socially and technologically, putting it all together, this is a quantum jump. We humans, according to her, who are living through this period of transition on the planet, are potentially an emerging new species. We need to know our own story of creation, and that we're part of it. And we need to know that we're an "emergent human," and that our growth potential literally has no limit. Part of this is that we need to learn co-creative relationships, and how to find our deep life purpose.

The concept of finding vocation is part of the emergent species. Women are shifting from maximum procreation to co-creation, to an expansion of creativity. As we move into that kind of action, we seek to model the changes we would like to see in the world by the way we create. We don't just create more bureaucracies, and more competition and more violence. We want to go out and create what Hubbard calls "Resonant Cores"–connecting to the heart with one another. Then the last thing is, we need to develop processes for social synergy and co-creation. "In Santa Barbara, we're learning all of this, and we're aiming at a community-wide synergistic event, with a local "Peace Room." The Peace Room is an idea I used when I was running for vice-president. Basically, it's a new social function that scans or maps and communicates what's emergent, what's working, what's innovative, what's already transforming the world."

The Peace Room is the opposite of the war room. They are designing it now in Santa Barbara, which has self-selected to be a prototype community, to see how this actually works. She has been carrying these ideas for many years, but what she realized, when the community responded, is that it takes whole communities to ground the idea of this new world view. It's not just self-help. It's not just social action, it's a whole system transition. That's what they are doing there creating a vocation to bring this into the world, developing a team. As the team develops, the way they relate to each other, the way they do the work that they are called to do, they want to model the change. "In other words, it's the famous saying, "Be the change you'd like to see." And we don't mean just personally. First of all, in small groups, and eventually in communities. If the community can be the change it wants to see, that's the most effective thing it can do."

Hubbard calls these synergistic events, which are like town meetings in the round. Instead of having people voting on issues, they have people in circles by function, health, education, government, science, the arts, media, culture, saying what they want to create, and then matching needs and resources with each other to co-create at a community level. "We are designing that type of event along with a peace room, which would be a way for people to track and map what's actually working. I think my most important insight, that moved me from San Rafael to Santa Barbara, was that it takes a community to consciously evolve."

Hubbard believes it takes a community to bring forth the creative potential of its people. And the way nature has worked for billions of years, is through separate parts joining together, to form a greater whole, through synergy. Synergy doesn't mean that everybody has to become the same, or do the same thing. It means everybody gets to do more of what they are uniquely creative in, by interacting with other people doing the same. "This is my hypothesis. I tested it out during the 70s, in the inner city of Los Angeles, and in the nation of Jamaica on the beaches, with people who didn't know how to read. Also in sophisticated places, like Washington D.C. When you create an environment that facilitates synergy and co-creation, it's totally natural, because people need each other to create. And we ask people three simple questions, in every sector of the wheel. "What is your current passion to create? Where is the juice for you?" Number two, "What's blocking you?" And, number three, "What resources do you have to share?" And when they respond to those three questions, even at a table of ten, there will be people who have something, a resource to match the need. Then the different sectors join together, and present this to an assembly of the whole. Let's say the health group says, "You know, here's what we want to create. Here's our needs, here's our resources." Another sector will say, "We have a resource to meet that need." And before you know it, the whole thing is synergizing."

Hubbard has a website, www.cocreation.org, which is the beginning of the Peace Room. They ask people to put their projects into the peace room and then, as they develop that further, they will have instructions and guidance…how we're doing it, so that others can learn from them, and they can learn from them.

"We're discovering as we go, because we've attracted about 150 people to form a kind of team, who will be practising the resonant cores, and studying conscious evolution. And then, moving out into the community to find the growing edge in every field, and bring people into synergistic events. So we're going to connect that which is emergent. Connect that which is innovative. And it's through the increased interaction of that which is already emergent, that you take the leap. This doesn't mean just a well known artist, and leaders–it also means kids and older people, wherever they're at their creative edge. We want this to be very much grass-roots. Very open, with a wonderful diversity and mixture. It sounds like a good way of going about getting people to do more than dream about it. Everybody gets to do more of what their passion is. That's why it works so well.

There is a real disaster area, she says, called the "news." The headlines in the newspapers... If you didn't know that anything was emerging on this planet, you would think we're going to hell, and we're already there. To some degree, there is hell going on, on this planet. But under the surface of the dying cultures, where we have the vast military build up, and the ethnic cleanings, and the inequities which are horrible–everywhere there are green shoots of new ways of doing this, that are cooperative and loving. But they haven't shown up yet. So it's springtime on the planet, very early springtime, according to Hubbard. "The two things I think are missing are the linkages among that which is already emerging, and the consistent communication of it, not just as an isolated bit of good news, but as an emergent humanity. It has to have the dynamism of the emergence, of what has been longed for by the human species, which is its own ability to connect with itself, with nature, and with spirit. And there are millions of people who are doing that now. I call these people a "new norm." We're not extraordinary spiritual geniuses. We are a whole crop of normal humans who are exhibiting some new characteristics."

■ ■ ■

5

BETTY BETHARDS

HEALING THROUGH DREAMS

Betty Bethards is a well known Mystic, Spiritual Healer and Meditation Teacher, and author of such books as The Dream Book, Ways to Awareness and Be Your Own Guru.

Bethards had two out-of-body experience which started her on her spiritual quest. With the first one, she had come home from playing bridge, went to bed about midnight, and woke up an hour later and was floating above her body. It was a dark room, but she could see her body down below her. It was very terrifying. She reached down and grabbed her body to pull herself back in. And a voice said to her, "You're going to be very sick with pneumonia; get to the doctor." So she woke up her husband and said, "I was floating above my body." He, a mathematician, said "That's alright honey, you'll be fine in the morning." So the next morning I said, "I want to go to the doctor, I have pneumonia." He said, "You don't look sick." I said, "I'm not, but I have pneumonia." So she went to the doctor and the doctor said "Betty, you don't even have a fever, there's no way that you have pneumonia." He wouldn't even give her an antibiotic. So she went to his partner and said, "Look, I've got pneumonia and I want a chest x-ray." He said, "you don't have pneumonia, lady", but he said it's important to acknowledge dreams. So he took two chest x-rays and sure enough, just starting up and down the left lung, was pneumonia. He couldn't believe it, but he said, "It's viral, go home, stay in bed and take aspirin." He wouldn't give me an antibiotic. I went home, but I didn't stay in bed because I didn't feel sick." Three days later, she was down with a temperature of 101,102,103…104 and 105!

And it went on and on. On the 10th day they wanted to hospitalize her but she said, "What are you going to give me?" The doctor said, "I'm going to give you pain killers and tranquilizers." I said, "I'm not in pain, I'm dying of fever. I can die cheaper at home." So she stayed home, and at the end of two weeks she was sitting on the couch leaning forward thinking "Boy, am I sick!" when she found herself in the dining room looking back at herself sitting on the couch, and said, "Wow, is she sick! I don't want to go back." And the Voice again said to her, a very powerful, loving voice (but it's one you trust and really listen to) "This is fine, you don't have to go back, but this is death if you choose to stay." It said, "You have 24 hours in which to have an antibiotic or you will have no choice and will have to come back." She said, "I don't want to come back." (You see it from a different perspective when you're out there.) So they started flashing my kids in front of her. The first one was 13. She said, "He'll be fine." The next one was 11. She said, "He'll be fine." Next one was 3 1/2. She said, "He'll be fine." The last one was 18 months and she said, "I have to go back." And then she was just instantly back in her body.

The interesting thing is, when she was across the room and looked down, she had a body–it had the same clothes on as the one on the coach did. But she was up by the chandelier, which meant she had to be at least 2 feet off the floor. So, this time when her husband walked in the door she said, "OK, this time I have 24 hours to get an antibiotic". She was living in Bellevue, Washington. She said, "You call every doctor in Seattle and get me an antibiotic. Now of course, I understand there's no accidents, or coincidences. We called the same clinic we'd been calling for two weeks, and this old Italian doctor answers and says, "Oh my God, get her into the car and I'll see her right now!" So he looked at the x-rays and said, "You've got to have an antibiotic right now." So her husband got the prescription. Her temperature broke to 101 that night. But it took her two months to get a clear chest x-ray.

"Once you know there's no death," she says, "you have to stop and say "Whoa! What am I doing here? Who in the hell am I?" And that's where you really stop and say, "OK...Jesus said it. He said, "The Kingdom of Heaven is within; go within and you'll know God." It's all inside of us. I had to wait two years before they started talking to me from the other side."

Her first out of body experience happened when she was asleep. The second it was daytime. Because this time she wasn't floating horizontally, she was standing up. She was in another room looking back at herself sitting on the couch. And if somebody lit a match at that instance, she could not have cared less. This is the thing you have to realize, she says. You don't care what happens to your body. It's like an old coat that you no longer need, and it has no meaning whatsoever to you.

People often dream about their health and often they dream about self-diagnosis, but she doesn't call it self-diagnosis. "I think God gives it to us. I hear the Voice. I mean the Voice is very accurate, very loud, but it's not me talking, I can tell you that. And I have heard the Voice many times. They do talk to people. I know Science likes to keep it medically-oriented, but I lecture in hospitals now. I teach healing to people, and I can tell you Science and Spirituality are going to merge. I've seen how far it's come in the 33 years I've been into it."

There's now prayer in over 50 of the medical schools in America, and they are taking diagnostic dreams more seriously too. And dreams are very accurate. Her book The Dream Book is an international best-seller.

This is what she explains in The Dream Book: Last night's dreams cover yesterday and today. Tonight's dreams cover today and tomorrow. They're all symbolic. If you take them literally, you're not going to think they mean anything. A car in a dream is always you. You always want to be at the wheel of a car and not in the back seat, not in the passenger seat, or you're not in control of your life. A house in a dream is always you. The bigger the building, the more potential you've got going. Each room is telling you something about yourself. In the kitchen, you are working on yourself. In the bathroom–shaving or showering– you are cleaning up your act. Or it means you need to clean up your act. If you're on the toilet, it's saying, would you let go of your stuff! Water is always the emotion. Anything flying, helicopter, UFO, airplane, is your creative energy. If the plane crashes then it's saying, "Boy, you've just lost your energy." And you can see it because it's covering where you are right now. Everybody in the dream is you, unless the person has died, then you're actually seeing that person. We're going out of the body at night. We're being taught and trained. In every dream you're falling, it's a bad landing, coming back in your Earth suit. If you jerk and you're dozing off, it's a bad takeoff. If you wake up in the middle night and you're paralyzed and you can't move, it's because you're not back in your Earth suit yet, you're just starting to come through the crown of your head. Take yourself down, and then you can move. Think yourself out and ask for the highest teaching you can be granted. And they will give you a one-liner that is so powerful you will be able to bring it back and remember it.

A man in a dream is always talking about your strong, assertive part. A woman in a dream is always your creative part. A child is always your child part. If you dream your child is dying in real life then it means, guess what–I've forgotten to make time for my inner child.

This knowledge really turns your head around. You begin to see that we all have a guardian angel standing over our right shoulder throughout our lives. We have a minimum of three teachers who walk through life with us. God doesn't trust you here alone. As we meditate and get our energy higher, we bring in more and more teachers. It's just like first grade, second grade, third grade...your perception about what life is changes, the higher your energy goes. If you're stuck in left brain thinking, you can't see the hand in front of your face. If you bring in a right brain oriented person, they can look at the problem and find it just like that–because the right brain is the imagination, is the bridge to God.

What about people who don't remember their dreams? They're too tired, according to Bethards. They're sleeping too heavily. If they nap they can catch the dream. They should sit on the side of the bed and say, "I will have a dream. I will remember the dream. I will wake up and write the dream down." Your mind is a computer, it will do whatever you tell it. So if you say that three times, real assertively, you'll find that every night you're going to remember your dreams.

The best teaching dreams happen between 3:00—5:00 am, and the one just upon awakening, Bethards asserts. You must write it down the minute you wake up or you're going to lose it. The dreams early in the night are just clearing house dreams–like clearing out the garbage in the dream of the day, seeing what you've let go of. All dreams are positive, but a nightmare will scare you to death so you'll remember it. Nice dreams go in one ear and out the other. We think, "Isn't that lovely" and we don't remember one thing. But if God terrifies us, we're going to look at it.

People who meditate are able to remember their dreams more. But all forms of meditation open the five senses, bring in intuitive abilities, so there is no bad meditation. But if you meditate and you aren't learning how to close down, you're just going to open yourself to go up and down like a yo-yo, and set yourself up for panic attacks. She teaches Meditation and Prayer which is Affirmation, Visualization. God knows what you want, she says, but you have to ask to get it. Otherwise God becomes your co-dependent. And of course God is Love in all religions. Whether people believe in God or not doesn't matter.

Some people have been working on themselves for years, meditating and so forth but are still searching for more guidance. That is because they are intellectualizing on this...they get that Intellect fussing with their Intuition. That's what's getting in their way. She advises them to try her technique of meditation. "One of the easiest ways to meditate is make a 20 minute tape of your favorite songs by your favorite singer. (I love Celine Dion, or Barbara Streisand, heart singers.) Then you're not going to mind sitting there for 20 minutes because you're hearing your favorite songs. Usually ten minutes is 3 songs. Have your hands touching for the first 10 minutes, palms up for the second 10 minutes. Turn one palm up for a second and close your eyes and inhale deeply through your nose. Then exhale through the nose, clear to the base of the spine. This time when you inhale, feel the electricity going in your fingertips. When you exhale, feel it out the fingertips into the energy field. Can you feel that? That's what you're meditating for–the electrical energy. Every cell in your body is an individual atom held together by electromagnetic energy. It brings the endorphins up, which stops you from having pain. It's healing, changing every cell in the body, plus you're awakening new brain cells. If you awaken new brain cells, you don't need the others that are lost. Incidentally by meditating, you can create other physical changes. I'm 66, but I have bones 127.9% better than anyone my age. So it shows you that meditation does more, and my energy is better than 20 year olds. Nobody thinks I'm that age. They look at me and think, "Are you crazy? You can't be!" So you begin to see there's no such thing as age; it's where our energy is that determines how old we are. When your energy is high, you see things very quickly and very easily. Your intuition gets stronger and stronger. By closing down at the end of the meditation, means you close your hands in a fist and feel a balloon of white light form around you. You could feel the electricity right? Close your eyes for a second now. Feel your energy field. Now think of a time when you were depressed. Feel what it feels like. Now think of one of the happiest times in your life. Feel what it feels like. You don't even think of it; it's just automatically happening. That energy comes pushing down heavily on you. When you think of the positive, it lightens right up. All we changed was our thoughts. So it's people's thoughts, words and actions that create their reality. This is all an illusion. We're only here to learn to know ourselves. Everybody thinks they're getting away with something–but it's all going down in your guardian angel's Book of Life for you, so that when you die you get to sit there and look at all of it and think, "Oh my God, we want to blame everybody else, but it's always us." Everything is us. If you go with that assumption, that "I created it," then you're going to be in good shape."

The only three tools anybody needs, she says, are free! They are: 20 minutes of meditation once a day, at least three hours of sleep–the dreams start coming through then–and then Affirmation and Visualization. Use your own mind; heal yourself. We're all a mirror for other people to see themselves in. Anything anybody is criticizing us for has nothing to do with us. This way there's no point in reacting or getting mad. Does that make sense? It changes your life.

"My Guide says don't get hung up on dependency on anything. Don't concentrate on the visuals, then. So when people are listening to music on a tape, they are doing this with their eyes closed. What you're trying to do is shut the mind up. The mind won't turn off, it has to go to one point. If you listen to the words of a singer, you're staying with the singer all the way through the 20 minutes. The mind is not there jumping around, thinking "I should be doing this, I could be doing that, I don't want to sit here." All that stuff doesn't enter your thoughts because you're tricking your mind, because it loves the song. You can see this with puberty. The minute kids start coming into puberty, they'll all reach for their Walkman's or headphones or something. It keeps the feelings up. Kundalini comes up powerfully twice in our life: at 14 we call it puberty; at 49 we call it menopause. Forty-nine is the greatest transitional time of our lives. It takes us out. It's like we no longer have to take care of others; we can stop and take our gifts to that highest point."

So obviously people influence their health with their thoughts, according to Bethards. Medicine is fine, but 96% of all illnesses are caused by thoughts. We get sick in the chakra where we hold the stress in. Second chakra, you'll set up prostate trouble, colitis, or female problems. That's usually due to people not using their sexual energy–trying to turn the sexual energy off. Third chakra is the solar plexus, which is everybody's fear/worry center. If you're reacting in your third or fourth chakra–fourth is empathizing with everybody, third is fear or worry–you want to get up to the Third Eye. If you're finding yourself reacting, take a slow deep breath through the nose and exhale through the nose and kick that energy right up to the Third Eye and say, "Wow! how did they just nail me?"

And look and see what it is. We're only running 5 or 6 lessons on ourselves in this lifetime, she says. That's where we get in trouble–the same dumb number over and over and over again. "That's why I want to stop and see what it is. Fear of abandonment is everybody's number. But of course, you can't be abandoned unless you abandon yourself, because your teachers are always standing there, loving you unconditionally. God loves you unconditionally. But if I don't love myself, I'm going to block anybody else loving me. This is why Self-love, is so important, because we really can't love anyone else if we don't love ourselves."

Everyone has latent intuition and spirituality. "Look at kids the first 7 years of their lives. They can psyche you right out. They're going strictly by the right brain, which is the God's eye, the intuition, the imagination. Around second grade or age 7 they start developing the use of reading, writing and arithmetic, the left brain, and that's where we start losing the right brain. A lot of people are creative, so they stay with it through different creative talents that they enjoy, but a lot of them lose it right there at age 7. Ages 14—21 is all physical growth, and 21—28 is all emotional growth. The 21-28 are the hardest 7 years, but 14—21 is no picnic."

Meditation is what helps me, she says. That's the spiritual journey. You never stop growing. I'm a mystic... You want to keep going to the mystical. So there's a difference between mystic and psychic. A mystic takes self-responsibility for all their thought, words and actions. A Mystic works hand in hand with God in order to change their lives, to rid themselves of all fear, to help their fellow man in a much higher way. Whereas everybody is psychic. They're channels–only as good as the person behind it, that they have coming through them. Everybody can get their own answers. Why should you pay somebody else for it?

There's a saying that when the student is ready, the master will come. They watch your energy field. By meditating you are constantly increasing the energy field. Teachers will lower their energy only to a certain point; you must earn them. You want to keep going from second grade teachings to third grade to fourth to fifth. "I've been in it for 33 years, and I can never know it all. And I'll tell you, I know more than probably 99% of people out there. You should take what feels right from me or any other teacher. Your gut will tell you what's right."

If a person wants to channel, it is the same preparation as meditation, she insists. You can't do it without preparation. You're not going to get very high energy. Your accuracy won't be good. We're just a pipe they channel through.

■ ■ ■

6

Caroline Myss

INTUITIVE HEALING

Caroline Myss, Ph.D. is Medical Intuitive and best-selling author of Anatomy of the Spirit, Energy Anatomy and co-author of The Creation of Health. She is a pioneer in the field of energy medicine and human consciousness, and a respected figure in the field of holistic medicine. She holds degrees in Journalism, Theology and Intuition & Energy Medicine, and is the author of many best-selling books, tape sets, videos and the PBS television special Why People Don't Heal and How They Can. Her work with Norman Shealy, M.D., a Harvard-trained neurosurgeon, has helped define how stress and emotion contribute to the formation of disease.

'Medical Intuitive' for Caroline Myss is a capacity to interpret the data in the human energy system, and apply that to assessing a person's health. Data includes emotional information, and fundamentally, one's biographical background. Which is why she teaches that your biography becomes your biology. For her, most of the data that is contained in your cell memory, and in your energetic field, is able to be picked up. The dominant energy patterns that are contributing to the stress in a human being, are able to be picked up, if a person is open enough. And so, for Myss, as a medical intuitive, that's where she focuses her attention. That's what the skill is all about, she claims.

Intuition to Myss is simply a skill. It's a fundamental survival skill, that is inherent in everyone's psyche. It's as simple as that. It's not different from the skill to digest food. Spirituality on the other hand, is a chosen path of developing intimate relationships with God. It's chosen, it's nurtured, and it's optional. Whereas intuition–it's there whether or not you have any consciousness about it at all. It's simply a natural survival skill. It is one of the senses. It's a survival sense. It falls under that category. "It's not a big deal. It's not a gift. You don't have to meditate for it. You don't have to snort tofu, any of this nonsense. It's gotten all the wrong press, because it's been put in the wrong category. Which is that it's extraordinary, when nothing could be more ordinary, she stresses."

Myss claims intuition is not metaphysical. It's quite physical. It's totally a physical skill. How does she perceive the chakra system which she uses in her intuitive healing? "It's not a five sensory realm. So, how I perceive the human energy system, is not five sensory at all. And it's not in auric fields. It's none of that stuff. I'm quite bland when it's come to drama in this field. I simply receive an impression. An impression comes very rapidly to me. I've often described it as a piece of ice — it has no feeling. It's very rapid, like an electrical shock, but without the shock. And once I start to have actual feeling sensations, then so far as I'm concerned, my readings become contaminated. So for me the information has to remain incredibly neutral. It's what I would call 'ice-like' information. I receive very rapid impressions. I don't have to sit there and concentrate. Because, if I start to really focus, my conscious mind begins to apply data, which is not accurate."

It's more like an antenna. It's not visual. She doesn't see discoloration in different chakras. She doesn't see any of that. "I think there are different layers to our being, yes. But, it's not unlike a layer cake. They're all the same things. And they're all different functions. One has a more practical survival level, that's the mind function. The heart function obviously has an internal level that has to do with the quality of developing perceptions, feelings, the self. And the spirit level has to do with the pondering part of our lives, the unanswerable questions. The "why I am here" kind of question. These are the unanswerables, they're meant to be pondered but never answered. And that's the province of what I would call the soul. The spirit for me is the eternal self. And when one incarnates, an aspect comes with that incarnation, that's called the soul. And together the mind, the emotional body, and the soul form the energy field that lives within this thing called the human body.

Certain forms of healing, like, Bach flower remedies, for instance, can work on the emotional level before disease will get down into the physical. Myss perceives disease as something that condenses from spirit down through these layers until it gets to the dense part. But, it's not just disease. I think every part of our lives begins at an energetic level. Like creativity. You can't separate anything from that archetypal process. So it would not be any different for illnesses. There is a belief pattern, that's very prevalent now in our holistic society, That illness is caused by negativity. No doubt, negativity is a major contributor. And a definite blockage to healing. But we cannot discount the reality of environmental causes, and DNA, and biological causes. We are also very presumptuous to negate the possibility that an illness may be a gift. It's a neutral experience. It should be viewed in some regard as no different than any other experience. For some people it's the most appropriate way for them to make choices–that would then take them down a different path in their life. In which case, was that a negative experience? Or was it a life-transforming one? That attitude about all illness being due to negativity, and negative in origin, is necessary to challenge.

"I don't think any of us can add energy to anybody. I think we can facilitate something profoundly energetic happening within a person. Helping them get in tune, as it were. But I think energy medicine is a field that is probably for me the most authentic level of medicine that there is, because it takes into account what I would call 'square one of creation'. Which is where energy meets the process of incarnating. So I think it is very much going to become the dominant practice of medicine in this next millennium. We have no other place to go but there."

Different energy medicines that are getting more known, Qi Gong, acupuncture, Jin Shin, flower essences, work on more subtle bodies, or layers, and perhaps can help balance people before they manifest gross physical diseases. They are a great assistance to that. But there's no such thing as a guarantee, she emphasises. She is not an opponent of allopathic medicine. She is its supporter. "And the reason is because I think that energy medicine, in my experience, when the field first emerged with a huge voice, it was claimed that it would outrun the capacity that allopathic medicine has to heal things. There was this belief that energy medicine could cure all forms of cancer, and this, that and the other. But it hasn't. It hasn't outrun allopathic medicine in the least. In fact, if you manage to heal yourself, you could get a good book contract out of this. That's how rare it is.

"One has to ponder what's the x factor that's missing in the healing ability of energy medicine. It is not what we thought it was cracked up to be, when we first began to turn our allegiance to that field. I have come to believe that energy medicine is a practice of healing that is dependent upon the energy of time. Whereas allopathic medicine uses linear time as a fundamental healing measure. Energy medicine needs to understand the dynamic of chiros time, that is the time without time. Ergo, I think that is one of the reasons, whether or not practitioners are aware of it." The focus is on letting go of one's past and forgiveness etc. The act of forgiveness is the act of returning to present time. And that's why when one has become a forgiving person, and has managed to let go of the past, what they've really done is they've shifted their relationship with time. Entering into the 'present time,' and that state of electricity is the one that accommodates energy medicine. That's the state that empowers energetic techniques.

That's the point at which aromatherapy shifts from being a perfume to actually being an energetic force. When you look at linear medicine, the whole thing is put in the language of time. Take these pills for six weeks. Cancer lasts seven years. These kinds of time elements that are built into an illness, is a very detrimental state of consciousness. But it is the consciousness we take into the energetic medical field. And these two are fundamentally incompatible. And that to myss is a reality that people have got to understand. That if they're going to use energy medicine, they had better learn to recognize their time zone, and their relationship to time.

Traditional age-old therapies focus on transcending chronos time, hour by hour clock time and on ascending into chiros time, trance time, no time. And that's why at that level, she says, you cannot apply the concept of time. The healing simply happens in what the aborigines call 'dream time', mystical time. Every tradition has a name for this non-tine zone. The Greeks called it chiros.

Regarding women's health questions, the most common areas of imbalance that you come across in women is the fear of not being able to survive as a single entity. The belief that they have to have a partner. Otherwise they feel quite vulnerable, according to Myss. "My workshops are 85% women on average. And I would say the majority of these women have been divorced at least once. And, many, many, are single. And not by choice, I might add. There are those who would make the statement, "I'm not interested in getting married again." And while that may be true, they are most certainly seeking somebody. Now, there's nothing wrong with wanting a partner. But what's worth questioning within oneself is if you're being motivated by weakness or fear, or if it's strength–because you want to engage with someone in a really dynamic relationship. What I see so often, is women using the phrase, "I need someone to take care of me." What do you mean take care of you? Why can't you take care of yourself?"

This psychological imbalance would perhaps leave one open to more physical imbalances because, what you do, if you get together with someone on the premise that, "I'm afraid of this life. So, will you take care of me?" You're setting yourself up for a fall. Because the survival archetype is an alive entity. Its personal agenda with every person is to empower them, so that they can stand up alone, as a functioning consciousness. Therefore, when you enter into anything, as a frightened being, that contract you make with another person out of fear, has to fall apart.

Women, however, are not more likely than men to hang onto wounds, and to use woundology to manipulate others around them, according to Myss.

Men very much can equally get into the little child, "Mommy, take care of me," thinking. Which is very indicative of unfinished business there. Being in the wounded psyche, it shows up differently. But that talent is not sexist. Though it is more acceptable in our culture for women to share and discuss wounds than it is for men. Men make a big deal. They get applauded if they stand up and say they're in men's groups.

When it is acceptable to share and discuss wounds, potentially, it holds everything that can empower someone. "If a woman walks in a group of battered women and says, "I've spent the last 20 years getting the hell beat out of me." And the other women say, "Me too, and guess what, it's not your fault. And you haven't done anything wrong. And in fact, you better not take that anymore." And all of a sudden this women begins to wake up, and recognize she's married to a bully. And one day she whacks him with a frying pan, and walks out of there. That woman's on her way to health. So there's a lot of healing that comes from these groups. But make no mistake, they could also come to a standstill. Once you become part of a healing group, it can feel like you're supposed to stay in that group, rather than utilize it for your healing, and then move on. As if to declare, "Okay, I am healed from that. And now I'm moving on. And I appreciate the support, but now I can support myself." But, if it happens that a person gets so cozy in that group, and begins to rely on those wounds–then you've got a problem. You've got a whole different illness going on, wound manipulation. It's what I call woundology."

The increased statistics in breast and ovarian cancer seem to indicate to Myss that most of the women who are most vulnerable, or growing in vulnerability are yuppies. Women who fall into the, "I can do everything," status. "I can be the perfect mother, and a full-time career woman, and the gorgeous wife, and endless socialite..." The women with high social pressure seem to be amongst the strongest carriers of the possibility of breast cancer. There are also other categories. Women who's responsibility for family seems to fall dominantly on themselves. Often there is a neglect factor, where they don't get any nurturing in return. The bottom line is self-care. When there is a dearth of self-care, that's a set up for illness.

What is happening across the board is that the recognition that emotions, and the spirit and soul play a fundamental part in the art of healing. Women most certainly carry a more sympathetic heart in the traditional, classic sense–the mother archetype. They have been given the role to carry the heart energy of the human community, whereas men carry the survival energy. But the paradigm of science medicine is being re-shaped to include the soul. And for that reason, a paradigm is shifting, which is allowing the heart to come into it. And that's women.

Science is a vehicle that has taken the heart out of healing. Not men, but science. Had it been women 200 years ago who were dominating the field when science came in, they might have done the same thing, because it was a force of evolution, in which science took hold and re-shaped this vehicle called healing. And now it's simply time for the heart to move back into that science, and merge it into another one.

The most important recent developments in alternative medicine is just the general open-mindedness now. And the fact that it's penetrated mainstream–whether or not the public would call it that. From all of these exercise commercials, to eat a healthy diet, to menus in restaurants, that are marked "healthy choice." All of that...it's penetrated, it's made its way into the backbone of culture now. And that is the major achievement. It's now become the foundation. We are re-shaping our culture around what it means to take responsibility for health. That you have to exercise, do this, do that, it's everywhere. Nike stock has earned its power in society based on the holistic health movement.

Dr. Norm Shealy and Carolyne Myss have founded the Institute for the Science of Medical Intuition and plan to begin their classes officially. They have got their Ph.D. programme in medical intuition accredited nationally through the English/Australian Commonwealth. The programme will lead to the licensing and Ph.D. of medical intuitives. There'll be a long programme. It includes residencies with physicians that would be available to someone who's living and practising in USA.

■ ■ ■

7

CHOA KOK SUI

PRANIC HEALING

Pranic healing is an ancient healing practice popularised in modern times by a Filipino, Choa Kok Sui who has treated numerous people and established a network of pranic healers around the world. He has published several books in which he explains this theory and practice: 1) The Ancient Science and Art of Pranic Healing; 2) Advanced Pranic Healing; 3) Pranic Psychotherapy.

Pranic Healing Theory divides the human body into the physical visible body and the invisible energy body called the bioplasmic body. Pranic healing utilises prana or ki to heal the physical body. It also involves the manipulation of the ki and the bioplasmic matter in the patient. Pranic healing can achieve the following results according to Choa Kok Sui:

1. "It can help parents bring down the temperature of their children suffering from high fever in just a few hours and heal them in a day or two in most cases;
2. It can relieve headaches gas pains tooth aches and muscle pains alsost immediately in most cases;
3. Cough and cold can usually be cured in a day or two. Lose bowel movement can be healed in a few hours in most cases;
4. Most illnesses such eye, liver, kidney and heart problems can be relieved in a few sessions and healed in a few months in many cases;
5. It increases the rate of healing by three times or more than the normal rate of healing. All these assume that the healer has attained a certain degree of proficiency."

Chakras or whirling energy centres are important parts of the bioplasmic body. They control and energise the major and vital organs of the physical body. There are altogether eleven chakras in the human body. These are:

1. Basic chakra (located in the base of the spine)
2. Sex chakra (pubic area)
3. Meng Mein chakra (back of the navel)
4. Navel chakra (navel)
5. Spleen chakra (between the solar plexus and the navel chakra)
6. Solar plexus chakra (solar plexus)
7. Heart chakra (centre of the chest)
8. Throat chakra (centre of the throat)
9. Ajna chakra (between the brows)
10. Forehead chakra (centre of the forehead)
11. Crown chakra (crown of the head)

In pranic healing external and internal factors should be taken into consideration. External factors are physical factors which contribute to diseases, like bacteria, malnutrition, toxins, pollutants, lack of exercise, poor breathing habit, insufficient water intake, while internal factors are emotional and bioplasmic like negative emotions blocked meridians or chakra channels pranic depletion and congestion and chakra malfunctioning.

Two basic principles govern pranic healing, the cleansing and energising of the patient's bio-plasmic body with prana or ki. By cleansing or removing the diseased bioplasmic matter from the affected chakra and the diseased organ, and secondly by energising these affected parts with sufficient prana or ki, healing is achieved.

There are seven basic techniques followed in the practice of elementary pranic healing according to Choa Kok Sui: 1) sensitising the hands; 2) scanning the inner aura 3) sweeping or cleansing, general and localised; 4)increasing the receptivity of the patient; 5) energising with prana through the hand chakras technique by a) drawing in prana and b) projecting prana; 6) stabilizing the projected prana; releasing the projected pranic healing energy.

All these have been tried and tested and most people are able to produce positive results in just a few sessions by properly following the instructions, according to Choa Kok Sui, provided you maintain an open mind and persevere.

Sensitising the Hands

1. Place your hands about 3 inches apart facing each other. Do not tense just relax;
2. Concentrate on feeling the centres of your palms. Try to be aware of the centres of your palms for about 5 to 10 minutes while you inhale and exhale slowly and rhythmically. Concentration is made easier if you press the centre of your palms with your thumbs before starting. Concentration on the centre of the palms activates the hand chakras thereby sensitizing the hands that is enabling them to feel the pranic energy or matter. About 80 to 90% of those following this procedure will be able to feel a tingling sensation, heat, pressure, or rhythmic pulsation, between the palms at the first try. It is important to feel the pressure or rhythmic pulsation.
3. Proceed immediately to scanning (described below) after sensitizing your hands;
4. Practise sensitizing your hands for about a month. As a rule your hands should be more or less permanently sensitised after a month of practice.
5. Do not be discouraged if your don't feel anything after your first try. Continue your practice. It is likely that you will be able to feel these subtle sensations by the fourth session. It is essential to keep an open mind and concentrate on the procedure.

Scanning

In scanning it is helpful but not essential to first learn how to feel the size and shape of the outer and health auras before scanning the inner aura. This makes the hands more sensitive. In healing we are primarily interested in scanning the inner aura through which the trouble spots can be located. When scanning withyou hands always concentrate on the centres of your palms,thereby activating and further enhancing the activation of the hand chakras.

Procedure for Scanning the Outer Aura

1. Stand about four metres away from your subject with your palms facing your subject and your arms slightly outstretched.

2. Slowly walk towards the subject, simultaneously try to feel with your sensitised hands the subject's outer aura. Concentrate on the centres of your palms when scanning.
3. Stop when you feel heat, a tingling sensation or a slight pressure. You are now feeling the outer aura. Try feeling the size and shape of the outer aura, its width from head to waist, waist to feet and front to back. Usually it feels like an inverted egg, wider at the top then at the bottom.
4. It is essential that you gradually become aware of the aura in terms of its pressure so as to be more accurate in finding out the widths of the outer, health and inner auras.
5. The outer aura is usually about one meter in radius but sometimes it can be more than two metres wide. Some hyperactive children have outer auras as wide as three metres.

Scanning the Health Aura

1. Having determined the size and shape of the outer aura move forward gradually still retaining the earlier position.
2. Stop as soon as you feel the subtle sensation again. These may be slightly more intense sensations. It is the Health aura that you are sensing now. Try to feel its size and shape. The average health aura is about two feet wide. When a person is ill his health aura is reduced in size to as little as 12 inches or less. But a healthy and energetic person's health aura may be as wide as three feet or more, feeling like a tapering cylinder wider at the top than at the bottom.

Scanning the Inner Aura

1. Proceed to feel the inner aura with one or both hands. Move your hands slowly and slightly back and forth to feel the inner aura which is usually about five feet in diameter. Concentrate on the centres of your palms when you are scanning so that the hand chakras may be further sensitised to subtle energy or matter.
2. Scan the subject from head to foot and front to back. Scan the right and the left sides. When the inner aura of the right and left sides of the body are scanned they should have about the same thickness. If one side is bigger or smaller than the other, then there is something wrong with it.

3. Special attention should be paid to the major chakras, that is the vital organs and the spine. Sometimes a portion of the spine is either congested or depleted even if the patient has no back complaints.
4. While scanning the throat area the chin should be raised to get a more accurate scanning, because the inner aura of the chin can interfere with the actual condition of the throat.
5. Scan the lungs from the back or the sides rather than the front to get accurate results.
6. Pay special attention to the solar plexus since many diseases of emotional origin affect the solar plexus chakra.

Interpretation of Inner Aura Scanning Results

1. While you scan your patient you may notice hollows or protrusions in some areas of the patient's inner aura. Hollows are caused by pranic depletion. Usually because the surrounding meridians or chakra channels are partially or severely blocked, preventing fresh prana from elsewhere to flow freely and vitalise the depleted part. In pranic depletion the chakra in question is depleted and filled with dirty diseased bioplasmic matter and is also usually partially underactivated.
2. When the area protrudes, it means there is pranic or bioplasmic congestion. Excess prana and bioplasmic matter, in the area in question cause the surrounding meridians to be blocked so that the excess prana and bio-plasmic matter cannot flow out freely. The affected chakra filled with diseased bioplasmic matter is usually over activated.
3. Some organ of the body may be affected by both pranic congestion and depletion simultaneously. This means that a portion of the affected organ is hollow while another is protruding.
4. The smaller the inner aura the more severe is the pranic depletion. The bigger the protrusion of the aura, the greater is the congestion of the affected part.
5. A part of the body may have a temporary pranic surplus in which case there is nothing wrong with the area as for example, a person who has been sitting down for a long time when scanned may show a big protrusin of the inner aura around the buttock area. But the condition normalises soon.
6. Similarly a part of the body may experience temporary pranic reduction with nothing wrong in it. For example a recent quarrel could have caused a temporary pranic reduction around the solar

plexus area, which a few hours rest will normalise. But continuous or habitual anger may cause chronic pranic depletion around the solar plexus resulting in abdominal ailments and even heart disease.

7. The physical condition of the patient should be observed carefully and the patient questioned exhaustively before jumping to any conclusion.
8. Diseases manifest themselves first on the bioplasmic body before being experienced by the physical body. Therefore pranic healing should be applied to the disease before it could be manifested physically.

Sweeping

Sweeping is used as a cleansing technique but can also be used for energising and distributing excess prana. Cleansing done for the whole bio-plasmic body is termed general sweeping and when done on specific parts of the body is called localised sweeping. Both hands are used in sweeping, sometimes held in cup hand position and other times in spread-finger position. These positions are used alternately. The cupped hand position is effective for removing the deceased bio-plasmic matter while the spread –finger position is appropriate for combing and disentangling the health rays.

Localised sweeping: This is done by 1) placing your one or both hands above the affected area. Concentrate on your hand and on the affected organ. Then slowly sweep away the deceased bioplasmic matter as if cleaning a dirty object with your hand; 2) strongly flicking your hand to throw away the dirty bioplasmic matter; 3) the sweeping movements can be carried out vertically, horizontally diagonally or in an 'L' shaped movement.; 4) for simple ailments localised sweeping should be done twenty to thirty times over the affected organ. Often the patient will feel partial or complete relief. This is a useful practice in treating stomach pain loose bowel movement and headaches; 5) in case of more severe ailments the number of localised sweeping treatments should be increased. In case of cyst localised sweeping carried out fifty times is appropriate; in case of acute hepatitis about hundred or more sweepings may be necessary; in case of tumour or cancer it will have to be performed 300 to 500 times; 6) experienced and proficient pranic healers are able to get effective results with greatly reduced number of sweeping movements.

Sweeping is very easily learnt by most people. They should however take care that in localised sweeping the diseased bioplasmic matter is not transferred from one part of the body to another. In such a situation localised sweeping needs to be applied on the newly affected area.

General sweeping is done with a series of downward sweeping movements only. Here you start from the head down to the feet. Upwards sweeping movements are not used in cleansing but to reawaken patients who may have fallen asleep or may have grown drowsy. In this case you start from the feet and go up to the head.

The General Sweeping Procedure is as Follows:

1. Cup your hands and place them six inches above the head of the patient. Don't touch the patient. Maintain a minimum distance of about two inches between your patient's body and your hands;
2. With your hands still cupped sweep your hands slowly downward. From head to foot. Slowly raise your hands and strongly flick them downwards to throw away the dirty diseased bioplasmic matter. This avoids recontaminating the patient with the diseased matter as also contaminating yourself;
3. Repeat the procedure (2) with spread –finger position instead of the cupped hand position. This disentangles and strenghtens the health rays and is called combing;
4. Repeat the whole process as in no. (2) and (3) to the sides of the patient.
5. Repeat the downward sweeping on the back of the patient. Using the same procedure as in nos. 2, 3 and 4;
6. It is essential to concentrate on the intention to remove the diseased bioplasmic matter. Otherwise the sweeping becomes less effective and more time consuming. With practice you can effectively used the sweeping movement with great ease and minimum effort.
7. After the downward sweeping some patients sometime become sleepy, in which case a few upward sweeping movements will reawaken the patient. But do not apply the upward sweeping movement before applying the downward sweeping movement which may result in the diseased bioplasmic matter getting stuck in the head area and worsening his condition.

Disposal of Bioplasmic Waste

The diseased bioplasmic matter has to be properly disposed of in order to maintain the premises bioplasmically clean and avoid contaminating yourself and other patients, unless the diseased bioplasmic matter is definitely disposed of there is a possibility it may go back to the patient because it is connected to the patient by bioplasmic threads,

So a bioplasmic waste disposal unit has to be made. And it can be done simply by putting about a litre of water into a bowl and adding a handful of salt into it. Water absorbs dirty bioplasmic matter and salt breaks it down. After every sweeping or cleansing procedure you should flick your hands towards the bioplasmic waste disposal bowl. Before healing, after sweeping and after energising wash both hands upto the elbow with water or salt water. Otherwise it may manifest itself as pain in your fingers, hands arms or you may contract the patient's symptoms.

Energising with Prana

When projecting prana into the patient's bioplasmic body, you should simultaneously draw in air prana from the surroundings. This will prevent draining or exhausting yourself and becoming susceptible to infections and diseases.

There are many ways of drawing prana and projecting it: among the safest and easiest ways is doing through the hand chakras. One of the hand chakras is used to draw in air prana and the other to project it on to the patient. Both left and right hand chakras can either predominantly draw in or project prana. The hand chakra is alternately drawing and projecting prana at a rapid rate. It is a matter of intention or will to make it draw more than it projects or vice versa. It can use either of the hands to draw or project the prana. For the right handed it is easier to draw in prana using the left hand chakra and to project it using the right hand chakra. The reverse is true for the left handed person.

Procedure

1. Press the centres of your palms to facilitate concentration;
2. The drawing in hand should be turned upwards while the projecting hand should be turned downwards or outwards that is away from your body;
3. Focus your attention for about 10 to 15 seconds on the centre of your palm that will be used for drawing in prana. This is partially to

activate the hand chakra, enhancing its ability to draw in prana. If you intend to draw in pranic energy through your left hand, then concentrate on its centre;

4. Place the other hand near the affected part of the patient's body and concentrate simultaneously on the centres of both hands. Maintain a distance of about 3 to 4 inches from the patient. Continue focusing your attention on the centres of your palms until the patient is sufficiently energised. In simple cases this may take about 5 –15 minutes for beginners;
5. There should be an initial intention to draw in prana through one hand chakra and to project it to the other. Once the initial intention has been established, there is no need to consciously maintain this intention. The position of the hands, initial intention and the concentration on the centre of the palms will cause prana to be drawn in automatically through one of the hand chakras and projected through the other.
6. Some healers commit the mistake of concentrating too much on the projecting hand and not enough on the receiving hand, and are not able to project enough pranic energy because they are not drawing enough of it. They also tend to become easily exhausted because they are using their own pranic energy instead of drawing it from the surroundings. Consequently you should concentrate more on the receiving hand than on the projecting hand to avoid becoming depleted;
7. When energising or projecting prana you should form an initial intention of directing the projected prana to the affected chakra and only then to the affected part. It is critically important that the projected prana be directed at the affected part since it will produce a much faster rate of relief and healing. Just energising the affected chakra without directing the pranic energy to the affected part will result in a slower distribution of prana from the treated chakra to the affected part, producing a slower rate of relief and healing ;
8. The right and left armpits should be slightly open to permit an easier flow of prana from one hand chakra to the other;
9. If you feel a slight pain or discomfort in your hand while energising, flick your hand to throw away the absorbed diseased bioplasmic matter. When energising the hand should be regularly flicked;

10. Energising should be continued till the treated part is sufficiently energised and you feel a slight repulsion from the treated part or a gradual cessation of flow of prana from your hand to the treated part. The flow of prana may feel like a warm or subtle moving current. For beginners energising 5—15 minutes for simple cases and about 30 minutes or more for more severe cases.
11. Cross check whether the treated area is sufficiently energised by simply rescanning the inner aura of the treated part. If it is not then energise further until the treated part has sufficient prana.
12. If the treated part is over energised apply distributive sweeping to prevent possible pranic congestion;
13. Prana can also be projected through the fingers or finger chakras rather than hand chakras. The prana coming out of the finger chakras is more intense and the patient may feel pain and a boring or penetrating sensation that is quite unnecessary. It is better to master energising through the hand chakras before trying to energise through the finger chakras.

One of the potential problems in pranic healing is the instability of the projected prana which tends to leak out gradually causing a recurrence of the illness. This can be prevented by stabilising the projected prana in two ways:

1. Complete all energising with prana by projecting blue prana. This is done by visualising and projecting light blue prana on the treated part;
2. Mentally instructing the projected prana to stabilize itself.

Now that you know to heal using pranic healing the following schedule should be maintained daily to acquire the necessary practice:

1. Sensitizing the hands – 5 to 10 minutes a day;
2. Scanning – 5 to 10 minutes a day;
3. General and localised sweeping 10 minutes a day.
4. Energising with prana – 10 minutes a day

This schedule should be maintained for at least 5 – 10 weeks to prepare yourself to heal somebody like your own child or others of simple ailments like fever, lose bowel movement, gas pain, muscle pain, insect and bug bites... This technique should preferably be applied on actual patients but if they are not available practise with a friend or relative.

It is advisable to learn to heal simple ailments at least thirty times before proceeding to treat more difficult cases. It is also advisable to study Choa Kok Sui's *The Ancient Science and Art of Pranic Healing*. Although the basics have been given in this chapter to enable you to start on your own, reading this book and his subsequent books, particularly *Advanced Pranic Healing* will give you much greater confidence. Both these books contain specific treatments for specific ailments besides the general treatment which has been given here in a condensed fashion.

■ ■ ■

8

Dan Millman

SPIRITUAL HEALING

Dan Millman is a former world champion athlete, college professor, and author whose Way of the Peaceful Warrior is a perennial on the human potential bestseller lists and has been translated into more than 20 languages. The book is a fictional account of a young man much like Millman, an athlete who meets a spiritual teacher and travels a fascinating road of self-discovery. Millman's book, Everyday Enlightenment: The Twelve Gateways to Personal Growth (Warner Books), is a programme of personal growth and self-knowledge, based on Millman's popular seminars.

Millman asserts that daily life is a perfect setting for spiritual practice, and that dealing with issues such as self-worth and self-sabotage are crucial aspects of spiritual development.

Part of the concept of the "peaceful warrior" comes out of his own peculiar life experience with the martial arts. He had come to appreciate not so much the fighting techniques, as the spirit of the martial arts. Ancient warriors, when facing the razor-sharp blade of a sword, knew that physical skill alone was important, but not enough, if the mind was in turmoil or the emotions embroiled. So the ancient warrior's training involved the balanced development and integration of body, mind, and emotion, forming a whole greater than the sum of its parts, or what is called spirit. When he began writing and expressing what he wanted to share, it was so holistic in nature that it was hard to have an umbrella or a container for it. It wasn't just about meditation, or just about physical training. That's when he went back to the idea of the warrior in each of us, the courageous part. But he knew it wasn't just about war and fighting, so the term came up, "peaceful warrior." That seemed to embrace the spirit of each one of us that involves having a warrior spirit and a loving heart.

Towards the end of his book, Everyday Enlightenment, Millman says that enlightened beings are "simply those willing to act in an enlightened way." "Each of us is traveling paths up a mountain to our potential . . . We've taken many paths. One of the major emphases of Everyday Enlightenment is that daily life is our spiritual practice. I'd like to share a story of a man who came up to me at a lecture and said, "I want to do more spiritual practices, but I have a family, a wife, three kids and a regular job." He and I chuckled about that later, because he came to realize that his wife and children and work were his spiritual practice, and that this was more challenging, and more fruitful in many ways than sitting in a cave meditating. I know, because I've done both. So for each of us, wherever we step, the path appears beneath our feet. The reason I wrote Everyday Enlightenment is to help people travel with a beacon or lantern, so they can see more clearly, and appreciate more clearly what their life experiences have to teach them."

In the book Millman presents twelve gateways to personal growth, and he strongly recommends that people do them in the order that they're presented, although, he says, in one sense, the order is arbitrary, in that anyone who opens the book and looks at the table of contents may see gateway number eight, "Face Your Fears," or number eleven, "Awaken Your Heart," or number five, "Tame Your Mind," or number four, "Manage Your Money," as the most critical one to them now. And they may jump right to that gateway.

He says he is not adamant about the order, but it seems to him that unless we deal with the first gateway, which is "Discover Your Worth," those with serious self-worth issues-and some with the highest vision and ideals have the biggest self-worth issues, because they never meet their standards-those of us who haven't addressed that tend to self-sabotage. They only will receive what they believe they deserve. And until they open their hands a little bit, and expand their arms, and are willing to receive more enlightenment, they won't make as good use of any of the other gateways to follow. It doesn't do any good to see some of the material of the second gateway, "Reclaim Your Will," until they're willing to allow abundance to enter their life, that is, spiritual abundance, not just material.

He makes a distinction between self-worth and self-esteem. "One of the biggest hurdles we need to overcome in order to learn is the hurdle called, "I know that already." Someone said, "The important thing is what we can learn after we know it all." Many people hear a term, and they say, "Oh, self-worth, I know about that. I read a book on self-esteem, and I went to a seminar. So I already know about this." Because self-esteem has been in the press so much, I wanted to differentiate it. Self-esteem is how we feel about ourselves. Do we like ourselves? Do we feel good about ourselves? Do we feel self-confident? Now, that can change from moment to moment. An athlete might feel confident on a playing field but have much less esteem on a dance floor or at a social gathering. So self-esteem can change depending on the circumstances."

Self-worth is a deeper value. It's largely subconscious. We know how we like ourselves at the moment, but our self-worth is more deep down, involving questions like: How deserving am I? How good a person am I? How much do I deserve? Consciously, we may feel we deserve the best, but maybe on some level that's not really what we're attracting into our lives. And that's why we need to explore it. Millman defines the subconscious as what is accessible to our conscious mind but still largely unexplored. So what the first gateway is designed to do is to take a look beyond self-esteem, to a more fundamental sense of how we value ourselves, respect ourselves, and how deserving we feel in life. The Indian saint Ramakrishna once said that the ocean can pour down from the sky, but if you're only holding a thimble that's all you're going to get. That's the essence, discovering how to expand a thimble into a mug, or a sink, or a bathtub, or a swimming pool. Doing nothing else in life except opening up and realizing our innate human worth, whether we felt we've earned it or not, can change our lives.

Millman believes one way to know someone's level of self-worth is to look at their life right now, in all areas. Many of us have the experience when something good happens, where we say, "This can't last." That's a self-worth issue. Or when we buy a new car or a new house, and it's so beautiful, and we go, "I don't know if I deserve this. I don't know if I fit here." Many of us have examples like that, he says. We pick a partner, maybe somebody very dynamic, or educated, or whatever, and we don't feel comfortable. We think it may be too much for us. So I think we select, and make choices in life, based upon our sense of self-worth, he concludes.

Often apparent bad luck sometimes turns out to be a blessing in disguise. In Millman's The Way of the Peaceful Warrior, there is a story about an old Chinese man and his son. The man had a very poor farm and had one single horse to pull the plow. The horse escaped from the corral and all the neighbors said it was such a misfortune. But the man just said, "Who knows?" Then the horse returned, bringing five wild stallions to the corral, and the neighbors said, "Great good fortune," and the farmer said, "Who knows?" Then, soon after, the young son was trying to tame one of the horses, and fell off and broke his leg. The neighbors came to commiserate, but the farmer still said, "Who knows?" Very soon after that, soldiers came to conscript all the young men for war, and they didn't take the farmer's son. So, good luck or bad luck, it's very difficult to determine. That's where fate comes in.

The second gateway is "Reclaim Your Will," and there he addresses that particular issue. Motivation is fickle; we don't feel motivated all the time. No one does. We can feel a lot of moments of motivation when we're excited about a project, but some days we don't feel motivated, and that's when will takes over. Will is like a loyal companion. If you have enough motivation, you don't need will. Millman trained in gymnastics for many years, four hours a day, six days a week. There was incredible exertion and risk. He was so motivated to do well, and that carried me. But those days came-when he was tired and feeling lazy and kind of burnt out-and that's when the will took over. That's ultimately what makes the difference. He likes to say he believes in St. Nike, "Just do it!"

When one awakens to the path of mastery in any field, one realizes, "What I'm doing is just like life." Whether it's learning gymnastics, or football, the person is developing internal resources that will carry them through life. Everything becomes a metaphor.

Several years ago Millman was watching Barbra Streisand on Lifestyles of the Rich and Famous. It became a turning point of sorts for him. "The first time I actually reflected upon my own attitudes toward money, I thought they were ultimate truths instead of just my own opinion. But I was watching, Lifestyles of the Rich and Famous, and Barbra Streisand was showing viewers through her house, which she had bought with the money she earned from her creative endeavours. She was showing a carpet, a gorgeous thick Persian wool rug, much bigger than any four rooms in our house. Beautifully designed, a one-of-a-kind carpet. I imagine this one carpet cost half of what our house cost. Then, when she lifted up the corner of the carpet, there was that same design on the marble floor beneath, so that when the carpet was being cleaned, she could still enjoy the design on the marble floor."

He had a negative emotional charge about that. It seemed to him ostentatious, in the context of how many people are struggling to make a living, and so on. He was offended by that show of wealth. And that would have been it, except a little later he realized that it's her money, and she earned it. And she needs to be able to choose, just like any of us should be able to choose, how we spend our money. It also struck him that Barbra Streisand, as he happened to know, gives more to charity than most of us may ever be able to donate. So it's an aesthetic choice she had made, but he was offended because of money. He realized in that moment that if that's how he felt about someone who was very wealthy, he certainly wasn't going to attract very much money. As a matter of fact, during that time he was mastering his poverty consciousness stage of life, working two jobs at seven dollars an hour. So that was a turning point, because he started examining his attitude toward money. One can go to every kind of seminar on abundance, franchising, or whatever else they want to do to make money, but if they feel doubt, and are real negative about it, they're unlikely to attract it, he says.

Millman claims that when he relates the twelve gateways to people, their eyes get wide, and they go, "Wow, Discover Your Worth, Manage Your Money, Energize Your Body, Change Your Mind." These sound very good, but whenever he comes down to the ninth gateway, "Illuminate Your Shadow," he usually gets a look of, "Huh?" People say the shadow sounds negative, evil, dark. Why would I want to illuminate it? Why would I want to deal with it? And yet, he claims, it can absolutely turn our lives around. "When we're infants, we're both light and shadow, both good and bad. Of course we're sweet, but we can also be bad. Ask a kitty cat that gets too close to the baby, and the child grabs at it.

They are powerful little beings. As we grow older, there are certain parts of ourselves that we don't approve of, or other people don't approve of. Maybe we grow up in a pacifist family and our aggressive side is skirted. Or we grow up as young gang members, and we push our sensitive, vulnerable side into our shadow. So there are aspects each of us have denied, where we've said, "That's not me." We've disowned parts of ourselves. What happens then is that we disown the power associated with it." By illuminating our shadow, several things happen. First, we end up finding much more compassion for other people. It's hard to point fingers at other people when we see all those shadowy aspects of ourselves, where we've lied, or cheated, or stolen people's time. Also, we create more energy in our lives, because we aren't using so much energy to defend our self-image. We become real and authentic, and much more powerful. So there's a lot to attract people to delving into the shadow.

Millman tells a story of a man who stands on a mountain top and cries to God, "Fill me full of light!" God replies, "I'm always filling you-but you keep leaking!" How do you plug those leaks? Millman claims we have twelve leaks, and that's why he wrote Everyday Enlightenment. Because there are many people who are specialists, who focus on one area of life. They may say meditation is the answer. "Nobody can deny that it's a very useful practice. But I know people who meditate a lot who practically go into catalepsy if their car breaks down, asking, "Where can I get the money, I'm broke!" So it's not just one practice that we need. We also have to learn to manage our money. And if we don't have an energized body, it's hard to have the energy to go out and create the wealth. So that's why I have twelve gateways, because it's not enough to deal with one area of life. It's as if life has twelve classes, and you have to complete all twelve in order to plug up the leaks."

What happens when we do so, he says. is that we free our attention, which has been trapped by worries about money, trapped by aches and pains in the body, trapped by wondering how to turn what we know into what we do. Once we free our attention, it rises naturally up to the higher levels of experience and awareness to the heart, where we feel more and more loving toward the world. Then we turn toward serving the world, which is the final gateway.

Although self-absorption is a common trait, Millman suggests it is a really useful phase in life, as long as it's not done to the exclusion of our relationships. "Know thyself" is advice given by the wise elders of antiquity. So there's a time when we need to look inside, and introspect, reflect upon ourselves, and find out who we are, but that's so we can then turn towards the world and bring more light and gift it to the world, to be more effective in service. Learning to give, to sacrifice, to help others, is not only joyous but an absolutely wonderful method of personal growth, according to Millman.

■ ■ ■

9

DEEPAK CHOPRA

HEALING THROUGH INTENTION

Deepak Chopra is a physician whose unhappiness with western medicine led him to search for an alternative. An endocrinologist who is a former Chief of Staff at the New England Memorial Hospital in Stoneham, Massachusetts, and who has taught at Tufts and Boston University Medical Schools, Dr. Chopra was introduced to the ancient methods of Indian healing, known as Ayurveda, by Maharishi Mahesh Yogi, the man who has done more than any other to bring traditional meditation to the West.

Chopra proved an apt student, and has become a master teacher as well. He is the founding president of the American Association of Ayurvedic Medicine, and has written and lectured widely, authoring the bestselling Quantum Healing, as well as Creating Health, Return of the Rishi, Perfect Health, Unconditional Life, and Ageless Body, Timeless Mind.

Dr. Chopra has initiated collaborations with medical associations in the Russia, Poland, Hungary and Brazil. He has spoken at the U.N. in New York, the World Health Organization in Geneva, the Soviet Academy of Sciences in Moscow, the Royal College of Physicians and Surgeons in Australia, the National Institutes of Health in Washington, and at medical schools worldwide.

Chopra has been instrumental in developing the practice of Ayurvedic medicine, which may well be the world's oldest living system of healing, in the United States. He is the Medical Director of the Sharp Institute for Human Potential and Mind-Body Medicine in La Jolla, California, and lectures and teaches worldwide.

Dr. Chopra found it frustrating to see patients again and again, and to keep giving them sleeping pills, tranquilizers and antibiotics, or their hypertension or ulcers, when you know you're not getting rid of the problem or disease. The word "cure" is not even used. You are just treating the patient. "Curing" is a term that all physicians avoid, he says. Doctors' training is not oriented towards that.

He began to advocate quantum healing which is healing the body-mind from a quantum level. That means from a level which is not manifest at a sensory level. Our bodies ultimately are fields of information, intelligence and energy. Quantum healing involves a shift in the fields of energy information, so as to bring about a correction in an idea that has gone wrong. So quantum healing involves healing one mode of consciousness, mind, to bring about changes in another mode of consciousness, body.

Meditation is a very important aspect of all the approaches that one can use in quantum healing, because it allows you to experience your own source, he says. When you experience your own source, you realize that you are not the patterns and eddies of desire and memory that flow and swirl in your consciousness. Although these patterns of desire and memory are the field of your manifestation, you are in fact not these swirling fluctuations of thought.

You are the thinker behind the thought, he says, the observer behind the observation, the flow of attention, the flow of awareness, the unbounded ocean of consciousness. When you have that on the experiential level, you spontaneously realize that you have choices, and that you can exercise these choices, not through some sheer will power but spontaneously.

The most harmful aspect of modern lifestyle is the loss of simplicity, and the loss of trust. The experience of alienation, fragmentation, isolation....this ultimately leads to all of the problems, like contamination of our environment, hostility towards each other, poor nutrition, and hard work, too much work . . . A work-oriented society, a success oriented society, in which we believe that somehow, material objects are the only source of our happiness.

I don't believe in the existence of time, he says. "That's one thing I have to tell you, and the other is that I don't take myself or what I am doing seriously. I believe in the ancient saying that this is a recreational universe, for those who want to share God's one great passion, beauty. I feel that I'm having a wonderful time. I don't look upon any of this as work. It's a source of great joy and happiness for me. I experience beauty in everything I do, and when I experience it emotionally, then I know intellectually that it must be the truth. So if I don't go to sleep by ten, it doesn't bother me, because I'm not tired. Most of my writing I do in planes, when I have plenty of time. I meditate whenever I have a chance, and that is actually more frequently than most of my patients meditate. I see patients about 50% of my time at this clinic. That too is a source of great joy to me, talking to people and interacting with people. In fact, I have learned more from my patients than from anybody else."

What has surprised Dr. Chopra most about Ayurveda is that when given insight, even a little bit of insight, patients find themselves empowered to do the impossible. Ayurveda is the science of life and it has a very basic, simple kind of approach, which is that we are part of the universe and the universe is intelligent and the human body is part of the cosmic body, and the human mind is part of the cosmic mind, and the atom and the universe are exactly the same thing but with different form, and the more we are in touch with this deeper reality, from where everything comes, the more we will be able to heal ourselves and at the same time heal our planet.

Chopra's father was a great source of inspiration for him, because he was such a wonderful father, who never in his life raised his voice. He brought up his two children as princes, told them that their birthright was to have all their desires fulfilled. He was a very strongly western-oriented doctor, however. He is a cardiologist, very well-known in India. But he is also a very fun-loving person. He still remembers going on vacations and picnics together, going to Shakespearian dramas together.

Chopra says he never wanted to be a doctor. He always wanted to be a writer and journalist, but when he got to college, he felt that he also had to be a doctor, because that was a very important part of his childhood experience, watching his father heal people. He has that ability. Not only as a great, great cardiologist, but also as someone who cares about his patients. Even when he is not in the hospital or office, he cares about them, he thinks about them, he talks about them to his children and his wife. Not giving away any confidential information, but just wondering how he can help them. He has always been a great source of inspiration.

He was not, however, inclined very favorably towards Ayurvedic medicine until the son introduced him to it. Now he is the most enthusiastic researcher on Ayurveda in India.

The research that interests Chopra most is the research on Panchakarma, which is the procedure for removing toxins from the body, and how it affects biological aging. And of course the research on the herbal preparations, which yield very interesting and previously unthought of ways of healing. Herbs don't usually work the way pharmaceutical compounds do, binding to receptor sites. They seem to be evoking and amplifying the body's own healing processes. They are much more gentle. That means they probably take longer. It's a much more gentle, a much more holistic, and a much more complete effect.

Most people think that aging is fatal and scientific data shows that that's not true. People don't die of old age, they die of diseases that accompany old age, and they are preventable, says Chopra. Most people think that aging is irreversible and we know that there are mechanisms even in the human machinery that allow for the reversal of aging, through correction of diet, through anti-oxidants, through removal of toxins from the body, through exercise, through yoga and breathing techniques, and through meditation. Most people believe that aging is normal but nobody defines what normal aging is. What we call normal may be the psychopathology of the average. Most people think that aging is genetic and yet if your parents lived to age 80+ that will add three years to your life.

The way you think, the way you behave, the way you eat, can influence your life by 30 to 50 years. Most people believe that aging is universal but there are biological organisms that never age. Most people believe that aging is painful and we know that pain is from diseases that are preventable, not from aging.

People have to change their concepts of aging and Chopra is not asking them to do so based on some fanciful notion but on scientific fact. When they change that, then their perception of aging will change and it will become clear to them how not to grow old and to become wiser, to become more creative, to become the springboard for creativity and affluence. Once your perception of the whole phenomenon changes, your reality will change because reality is nothing other than your perception of it.

He has stated that if we could effectively trigger the intention not to age, the body would carry it out automatically because intentions are the triggers for transformation in the body. If you want to wiggle your toes, you do it through intention. There are two components to biological information in the body, one is intention, the other is attention. So to go back to the example of wiggling your toes, the first thing that happens is that your attention goes there and the second thing is there is an intention, so this biological information with attention and intention is what biological information is given. Awareness that acts as biological information goes to components, then an informational component, and then there's a localizing component, and that's how the body behaves.

If you can wiggle your toes with the mere flicker of an intention, why can't you reset your biological clock? The reason most people can't do it is because, first, they never thought of it and, secondly, they think that certain things are easier to do than other things. For example, it is easier to wiggle the toes than to reset the biological clock, but that is just a belief that is rooted in superstition. If we could understand that the human body is a network of information and energy, then we would see that the same principles apply everywhere in the body.

It's the same mechanism in ageing, says Chopra . It's just that we have been indoctrinated into believing that some things are easier, some things are more difficult. Expectations determine outcome, always! In other words our bodies are the outpouring of our belief system and experiences, so if you are having the experience of anxiety, your body is making adrenalin and cortisone, if you are having the experience of tranquillity, your body starts making valium, if you are having the experience of exhilaration and joy, your body makes interleukins and interferons which are powerful anti-cancer drugs. So your body is constantly converting your experiences into molecules.

One person's enemy is another person's best friend. My favorite food might give you a rash, etc. Every experience that we have is unique to us because at some deep level we make an interpretation of it. Because the body is the end product of intelligence, how that intelligence shapes your reality will shape the reality of the body. The body is a field of ideas and it is a field of interpretations and when you change your experience of your own identity to a spiritual being, the body expresses the physical manifestation of that spiritual reality.

It is a very important component, to have passion, to have a dream, to have a purpose in life. And there are three components to that purpose, one is to find out who you really are, to discover God, the second is to serve other human beings, because we are here to do that and the third is to express your unique talents and when you are expressing your unique talents you lose track of time.

The only way you can do that is when you know that a part of yourself is in fact, forever. There is a part of yourself that is not subject to change, it is the silent witness behind the scenes. That is essentially your spirit, the spirit being an abstract but real force. It is as real as gravity. It is as real as time. It is incomprehensible. It is mysterious but it is powerful and it is eternal. It is without beginning, without ending. It has no dimensionality, it's spaceless, timeless, dimensionless, eternal, forever. When you can get in touch with that part of yourself, then you will in fact see that present moment existence, even an entire lifetime is nothing other than a flicker in eternity, a parenthesis in eternity, a little flash of a firefly in the middle of the night in the context of eternity. What happens with that knowledge, with that experience, is that you begin to experience mortality as quantified immortality, you begin to see time as quantified eternity and when you see it against the backdrop of who you really are, then the anxiety of daily existence disappears. So one ceases to be troubled as well as influenced by the trivial things of daily existence, the little hassles that create stress in most people.

So it becomes much more joyful and you realize that the present moment is as it should be, there is no other way. It is the culmination of all other moments and it is the central point of eternity. So you pay attention to what is in every moment. And when you do that, then you realize that the presence of God is everywhere. You have only to consciously embrace it in your attention. And that's what creates joyfulness. You have to know the reality and the reality is that we are eternal.

If you look at anything physical, you find out that at the quantum level, it is non-physical, says Chopra. The body is made up of atoms and subatomic particles that are moving at lightning speed around huge empty spaces and the body gives off fluctuations of energy and information in a huge void, so essentially your body is proportionately as void as intergalactic space, made out of nothing but the nothing is actually the source of information and energy. If you'd approach that level then you would realize that the body is a print out and by changing the software, by influencing the programming, and by getting in touch with the programme you can create a new body anytime you want.

Living in the present moment creates the experience of eternity. It is like every drop of water in an ocean contains the flavour of the whole ocean. So too every moment in time contains the flavour of eternity, if you could live in that moment, but most people do not live in the moment which is the only time they really have. They either live in the past or the future.

If you could live in the moment you would see the flavour of eternity and when you metabolize the experience of eternity your body doesn't age. Meditation lowers biological age by quieting the mind which then quiets the body and the less turbulent the body is, the more the self-repair, healing mechanisms get amplified. In fact, scientists have shown that the better your DNA, your genetic machinery is at healing itself, the longer you live. That's how meditation lowers biological age.

Deepak Chopra offers the following self-healing exercise: every day keep aside ten minutes during which you should close your eyes and ask yourself two questions: 1) Who am I? and 2) what do I want? Contemplate these two questions without actively seeking any answers, for just ten minutes a day, every day. He assures you your life will be transformed.

■ ■ ■

10

Dean Ornish

NATURAL HEALING OF HEART DISEASE

Dr. Dean Ornish is a trained medical doctor and renowned clinical researcher. Dr. Ornish is the founder of the Preventive Medicine Research Institute in Sausalito and the Center of Integrative Medicine at the University of California, San Francisco. He is the author of four best-selling books including Eat More, Weigh Less and Love & Survival. His work has been featured in virtually all major media, including Bill Moyer's PBS special "Healing and the Mind."

Dr. Ornish has done ground breaking research on the connections between diet, exercise and health. In his most recent book, Love and Survival, he focuses on emotional and spiritual heart disease. He claims it has always been part of his work, although most people tend to think of diet when they think about the work that he and his colleagues have been conducting. Clearly diet and exercise is important, he says. Stopping smoking is important. Managing stress is important. Equally important is addressing the psycho-social, emotional and spiritual connection in health and healing, which interact with these other factors. Awareness is the first step in healing, and he says he wrote Love & Survival in hopes of raising the awareness of how much these things matter — so that people could then begin to make changes, or would at least have the option to do so. Study after study has shown that people who feel lonely, depressed and isolated are many times more likely to die prematurely today, because they don't have a sense of love and connection with the community. Yet doctors don't learn this in their medical training. They tend to not value this in western culture. Dr. Ornish wrote this book in the hope that it would help people understand that these things really do matter —not just for the quality of our lives, but also for our survival, and not just a little bit, but a lot.

In the book Dr. Ornish mentions the concepts of love, intimacy and meaning: those are essential to his work. He says that they are the least understood, as well as the most important. In science, he says, we tend to focus on what we can measure, even though what we can measure may not necessarily be what is meaningful. Not everything that is meaningful is measurable. We tend to focus on cholesterol and blood pressure, things we can more easily measure even though that may not necessarily be what's most important. There is a wide body of evidence showing that people who feel lonely and depressed and isolated are 3 - 7 times more likely to get sick and die prematurely than those who have a sense of love and connection in the community. "I don't know of anything in medicine that has a more powerful impact across the board, not just with heart disease but also with most other illnesses." Researchers found in one study, for example, that by asking people about to go through open heart surgery (both men and women) two simple questions, the answers were powerful predictors of who was likely to survive six months later.

Researchers asked:1) "Do you draw strength from your faith?" Whatever that faith was did not matter. 2) "Are you a member of a group that gets together on a regular basis?" It could be church or synagogue, civic group or bowling league. What they found, was mind boggling: those who said "No" to those two questions, 21% had died within six months of the open heart surgery. This is compared to only 3% of those who said "Yes" to those questions, a seven-fold difference in mortality. Those who said "Yes" to one of the two questions had about a four-fold difference in mortality.

Dr. Ornish asserts he is unaware of anything else that is so powerfully predictive, and yet most surgeons don't bother to ask these questions to their patients because they don't realize how important they are. "You know you are dealing with something very powerful when these relatively crude measures of love and intimacy are so powerfully predictive of survival (just a few months later, or sometimes decades later). A bowling league is not the most intimate of life experiences, and yet look what a difference it makes in these people."

This is because of social bonding. When Dr. Ornish talks about intimacy, he doesn't just mean sexual or romantic intimacy, although those are nice forms of intimacy. Intimacy is anything that takes us out of the experience of feeling separate. Someone or something other than ourselves. It could be a lover, a friend, a relative, a community member; it could be a pet. It could be a spiritual or transcendent experience — feeling like a part of everything as opposed to feeling apart from everything. There are many pathways to intimacy. "I outline eight in the book. These are just eight of many, but eight that have been helpful to me in my own life as well as in the lives of many other people with whom I've worked with over the years. That these things matter is clear. Why they matter is a bit of a mystery, and in the final chapter of my book I interview 24 different people and ask them all the same question, "Why do you think isolation is such a powerful predictor of illness and suffering, while intimacy is powerfully healing?" They all started in different places within their own frame of reference, but they ended up in a place that was very similar. In most systems of healing other than Western medicine, there is a concept of vital energy, sometimes called chi, qi, prana, shakti, or kundalini, and the idea that we are all interconnected at some level."

You can cut yourself off from that interconnectedness through putting up walls, emotional defences for example, according to Dr. Ornish. Not that you shouldn't have some defences, but if they are always up and you have no one you trust enough to open up to, then those same walls that you think are protecting you are also isolating you. It takes energy to keep defences up but more importantly it is cutting you off from the energy that is already there between you and the rest of the world. It is a little like walking into a room that has lots of windows and it's a bright sunny day outside but you can close all the windows and shades and make the room dark. It is still bright outside but you have just cut yourself off from the source of light. Again, it's not that we shouldn't have emotional defences, but if you have no one to feel safe enough with to let them down, then they are always up. The paradox is in the name of protecting us they are actually isolating us. Isolation itself threatens our survival. The very thing that we think we are doing that's protecting us is the very thing that may be harming or maybe even killing us. Part of the value of science is to help raise the level of awareness to how much these things really matter. If we can understand how much they matter, then we can make different choices. There has been a radical shift in our culture in the last 50 years with the breakdown of the social network. You can give people a sense of connection and community. These things affect the quality of our lives — and our survival.

They also affect our behaviours. People that are lonely and depressed and isolated are much more likely to smoke, to overeat, to drink too much, to work too hard, to abuse drugs, to spend too much time on the internet, to watch too much television, and so on. So it's not enough to just give people information and expect them to change. We have to work at a deeper level.

If a person wants to make lifestyle changes it isn't necessarily easy. If you have a family to change for as well as yourself, Dr. Ornish urges forming a support group to help you. "In working with people over the years I ask them why do you smoke, or overeat, or drink too much, or work too hard, or do drugs, or spend too much time watching television or on the internet. These behaviours seem so maladaptive to me. They say, "You don't get it, these behaviors aren't maladaptive, they are very adaptive because they help me get through the day." For many people, just getting through the day is the most important thing. One woman said, "I have 20 friends in this one package of cigarettes. They are always there for me. Nobody else is. You want to take away my twenty friends? What are you going to give me instead?" People may use food to fill the void, or alcohol or other drugs to numb the pain. They work too hard to distract themselves from the pain, or watch too much television. We have lots of ways of numbing, killing, bypassing or distracting ourselves from pain. The pain isn't the problem, it's a messenger. It is saying, "Listen up, pay attention, you are not doing something that is in your best interest." If we just try to numb pain or kill it or bypass it without listening to it, then it is a little like clipping the wires to a fire alarm, and then going back to sleep while your house keeps burning down. The problem is still there and it just gets worse."

Ornish points out that pain can be a powerful catalyst for transformation. Change isn't easy. If you are in enough pain and the strategies for numbing, killing or bypassing it aren't working that well, then sometimes the idea of change becomes more appealing. You think, it might be hard to change but I am in so much pain I am ready to try just about anything. When people make these changes, and they see how much better they feel and how quickly it happens, they look back on the suffering itself as a blessing in disguise. They say things like "having a heart attack was the best thing that ever happened to me. It made such a powerful difference in my life. Had I not gone through that experience I never would have changed."

"Healing and curing are not the same," Dr. Ornish writes. "Disease and illness are not the same. Pain and suffering are not the same." Pain is a physiological process of your nerves transmitting information. Suffering is the experience of that. We've all had times when the same level of external stimulation may be perceived as much more painful than at other times. So we can't always control pain, but our experience of pain is something that is often affected by the amount of support that we have. The same is true for disease and illness. Disease is the physiological process. Illness is the experience of that. With illness, while no one searches for that or wants it, there can often be a transformative quality about it. Not that you would ever go up to somebody suffering and say, "Oh what a great opportunity you have to transform because you are sick." The proper response to that would be a punch in the nose! We don't look for suffering, but it's there. How we deal with it is something that we have much more control over than we might realize. The same is true for healing and curing. Curing is the physiological process of getting better. Healing is the process of becoming more whole. They often go together. "My colleagues and I at the non-profit Preventive Medical Research Institute have shown over the years that you can often reverse the progression of heart disease much more quickly than what we once realized. We can use high-tech, state-of-the-art measures to prove the power of very low-tech and low-cost interventions. We can show that there is actually an improvement in the underlying disease process. If you talk to the patients who go through our study, they'll say they first got interested because they wanted to get cured, but they stayed interested because of the healing end of it. They will say things like, " I am not as concerned that my arteries are more open, because I am more open. In other words, my relationships are better, my capacity to love myself and others is greatly improved. I am learning to quiet down in my mind and body so that I can re-experience inner sources of peace and joy and well-being."

It is not that anyone looks for pain or illness or suffering or disease, but they can be powerfully transformative. These aren't things doctors are trained to look for in Western medical training. Even if the disease doesn't get better physiologically, there can still be healing that occurs. Even in death there can be healing, in terms of the level of intimacy and inner peace that people have the potential to discover during these vulnerable moments.

Dr. Ornish in his book quotes from The Broken Heart by Dr. Lynch that says "There is a biological basis for a need to form loving human relationships." He emphasises that is how we've been able to survive as a species for so many years and warns that we ignore these fundamental human needs at our own peril. The need for love is a basic human need that's as fundamental as eating and breathing and sleeping. We don't generally realize how important these things are. We think that the time that we spend with our loved ones is what we do after we've done all the important stuff. We don't necessarily realize that it's the other way around. You work long hours, travel a lot and maybe spend a few precious minutes with your spouse or kids when you come home from work. It's like a luxury and yet we don't realize it's a basic fundamental human need. Here again, that's part of the value of science, which can help us understand and raise the level of awareness of how much these things matter so that at least we know we have a real choice there, and we're not just blundering into things out of ignorance.

Love seems to apply on many levels from politics and taking care of the environment to our own bodies. Part of the research that we are doing is trying to show that these approaches are both medically effective and even cost effective. "If I went to an insurance company or Medicare and said, "I want these people to open their heart," they would show me the door! But if I say, "Here are the arteriograms and the cardiac catscans, etc. all showing reversibility of heart disease. For every dollar you are spending (whether it's Mutual of Omaha or Blue Cross/Blue Shield or whatever company), we're saving several more immediately, they say, "Oh that's really great! Tell us more, and maybe we'll cover it." More than 40 insurance companies are paying for this programme and Medicare recently agreed to begin a demonstration project where they're going to cover 1,800 patients who go through the programme in the sites where he trains."

Dr. Ornish's programme for reversing heart disease is a low fat, whole foods, plant-based diet which includes fruits, vegetables, grains, beans, non-fat dairy, soy products, egg whites, to which is added oil, 3 or 4 grams a day of fish oil and flax seed oil. There's also moderate exercise, walking 30-60 minutes three times a week, stopping smoking, and a variety of stress managing techniques such as yoga, meditation, stretching, breathing, and relaxation techniques. There are also support groups for reversing heart disease. Plus some supplements and vitamins.

These are all listed on Dr. Ornish's web site (www.ornish.com which is part of webMD). The web site covers all the elements of the program: how to stay on the programme, the recipes, the vitamin and supplements he recommends — they're all there and available free of charge.

"I feel good about that because having really seen what a powerful difference changes in diet and lifestyle can make, it really provides an opportunity for us to make a difference."

■ ■ ■

11

HEALING THROUGH MUSIC

From the siren's serenade to sweeping national anthems or rousing gospel hymns, music has long claimed powers of temptation and salvation. The idea that music can affect healing and behavior is at least as old as the writings of Aristotle and Plato. Music has been embraced by the masses, chained to commercials selling chicken or sneakers, and still managed to maintain its beauty and mystique. Now science — the great explainer of many mysteries — has turned its inquisitive eye to harnessing music's magic.

Modern medicine has taken to heart what ancient peoples have practised for centuries. "Music therapy," according to Mathew Lee, Acting Director of the Rusk Institute in New York, "has been an invaluable tool with many of our rehabilitation patients. There is no question that the relationship of music and medicine will blossom because of the advent of previously unavailable techniques that can now show the effects of music."

Music therapy has been advancing as a profession and medical tool since the post World War I and II eras when community musicians began playing for thousands of veterans recovering from physical and emotional trauma. They discovered that music could help alleviate pain, calm or relax patients and counteract depression, and encourage movement as part of physical rehabilitation. The resulting successes led hospitals to call for the hiring of musicians. When it became apparent that the musicians needed some prior training, the demand grew for a college curriculum.

In 1944, Michigan State University established the world's first music therapy degree programme. Shortly afterwards in 1950, the National Association for Music Therapy was founded to help ensure that practising music therapists were qualified to heal. A music therapist is often part of a team of doctors, social workers, teachers, parents or psychologists which assesses the patient's or client's condition and sets the goals for recovery. A therapist, trained to anticipate how a certain type or application of music will affect behavior, will devise structured activities which could include singing, playing instruments, movement, composition, or listening. Although patients using music therapy may develop musical skills, the goal is not to train musicians, but to improve — through music — physical, social or emotional skills; to help people regain their health and speed recovery.

Dr. Oliver Sacks, in *Awakenings*, wrote, "I regard music therapy as a tool of great power in many neurological disorders — Parkinson's and Alzheimer's — because of its unique capacity to organize or reorganize cerebral function when it has been damaged." Sacks also reports that patients with neurological disorders who cannot talk or move are often able to sing, and sometimes even dance, to music. While music therapy may still be edging into public consciousness, many different populations are already benefiting from its application. Some schools have taken the lead in using the arts to improve students' ability to learn. They have begun to hire therapists or other specialists who use music to strengthen nonmusical areas such as communication, physical coordination, teamwork, or even math.The media spotlight has shone on studies which quantify the value of arts in education. According to the College Entrance Examination Board, students of the arts continue to outperform their non-arts peers on the Scholastic Assessment Test. In 1995, for example, SAT scores for students who studied the arts more than four years were 59 points higher on the verbal and 44 points higher on the math portion than students with no coursework or experience in the arts. Richard W. Riley, the U.S. Secretary of Education, commented, "The process of studying and creating art in all of its distinct forms defines those qualities that are at the heart of education reform in the 1990s — creativity, perseverance, a sense of standards, and above all, a striving for excellence."

Music therapy is also commonly found in nursing homes, where it is often incorporated into the daily schedule of activities. In the early 1980s, a music therapist who was working in a nursing home, says "Perhaps, my most valuable role was as a roving flutist. I played familiar hymns or old tunes to residents who were bedridden, severely depressed, or dying of cancer. Although a few of the nurses thought it was a frivolous venture at best, I found some of the elderly folks I visited were able to hum or sing along, and recall the times and family associated with the tune. These brief moments of recognition were a small yet vivid proof of connection."

While she didn't continue as a music therapist, she still finds the application of music to the science of healing a fascinating arena. If the value of music therapy is still being quantified, the stories of people who have been helped by music offer compelling testimony. Ida Goldman, a 90-year old woman who spoke at a U.S. Senate hearing, said, "Before I had surgery, they told me I could never walk again. But when I sat and listened to music, I forgot all about the pain." (Goldman walked with assistance during the hearing.) Recent research has pointed to the value of music and the arts in treating Alzheimer's disease, strokes and related dementias.

Carei Thomas, a jazz pianist in Minneapolis, woke from minor surgery in 1993 to near paralysis. Thomas was a victim of Guillain-Barre Syndrome, a rare inflammatory disorder of the nerves near the brain and spinal chord. Right from the beginning, his recovery was driven by music. Friends played for him in the hospital, a benefit was held by the arts community; and perhaps most importantly, Thomas' own desire to return to music and performing spurred major progress. He is now walking with canes and playing keyboard using his hands in a more percussive manner. He has also turned to spoken word performances.

As new research continues to back the value of music in therapy and areas including education and reform, the music therapy profession and its uses continue to expand. Therapists can be found in hospitals, nursing homes, treatment centres, psychiatric wards, prisons, group homes and schools. There are professional music therapy sites growing internationally including the Association of Professionals and Students of Music Therapy in Sao Paulo, Brazil, a Music Therapy Centre to be built in the southern Bosnian town of Mostar, and the 8th World Congress of Music Therapy held in July 2001, in Hamburg, Germany.

Healthy individuals are turning to drumming and playing other instruments to relieve stress and improve concentration. Listening to certain types of music can ease the delivery of babies or motivate people to exercise. Simply put, music can heal people.

■ ■ ■

12

INDIAN MASTERS

HEALING THROUGH MEDITATION

Numerous studies have proved that meditation enhances health overall, retarding aging. Here are some masters' prescriptions on how best to meditate.

Sitting Meditation

Classic sitting meditation is a vital part of all meditation traditions and has taken many forms, some more effective than others. Some traditional approaches demand that the student sit motionless for hours on end as if becoming a human statue is the key to enlightenment. A more scientific approach does not make the human body our enemy but rather works with our natural physiology to allow more intense meditation with less effort and discomfort. Masochism is not an effective path to self-realization and the macho slogan 'no pain, no gain' has no relevance to meditation.

Begin by finding a relatively quite place to meditate where you will not be disturbed. You can sit cross legged on a meditation pillow on the floor or in a comfortable chair. Eyes can be fully open, half open, or just slightly open letting in two small slits of light. Sitting meditation with the eyes fully closed, especially in a darkened room, presents fundamental physiological problems.

When you sit quietly with your eyes closed in darkness your brain interprets this situation as a signal to start shutting itself down for sleep. Sleep inducing hormones such as melatonin are released that make you drowsy at the same time your circulation and heart rate are reduced due to lack of movement. You feel as if swept away on a sea of quiet relaxation. This pleasant feeling may just be 'light sleep state hypnosis', not meditation.

Meditation means that you are relaxed as if sleeping but your consciousness is fully awake.

To achieve a positive combination of deep relaxation and heightened awareness keep your eyes open at least slightly. If your eyes are fully closed then the room must remain brightly lit so that some light passes through the eyelids. The second defence against sleepiness is to break up your meditation into three fifteen minute sessions that are easy for your body to tolerate. Sit quietly for fifteen minutes, then stand for two minutes, then sit for another fifteen minutes, then stand for two minutes, then sit for a final fifteen minute session. This 49 minute technique can be done once a day, twice a day, or even three times a day for intense practice. You can time yourself by making a tape recording with the sound of a bell or a gong to let you known when to stand up, sit down, and begin and end the meditation.

This technique largely eliminates the problem of cramps, soreness, and numbness in legs often experienced by meditation students attempting to sit for longer periods of time than the body was naturally made to sit. The standing breaks increase blood circulation which helps wakefulness. Comfort is maintained and we avoid the 'light sleep state hypnosis' problem mentioned earlier.

The transitions between sitting and standing in this method are an opportunity to practice meditation in action. Normally unless we are physically ill our waking lives are spent in motion and activity. Meditation must not be thought of as something that is done only in a physically rigid state far removed from the world of work and play. The goal is to become meditative continuously so that your very being becomes cosmically conscious permanently and irrevocably. So when you stand up and sit down during these meditation sessions feel the inner flow of meditation continue. Observe that your body is moving but your existential identity remains the same.

What do you do While Sitting?

The most basic approach to meditation is to relax, let go, and do nothing. Surrender to the moment and watch yourself as a 'silent witness'. If thoughts come to mind then observe the thoughts without adding to them by your active participation. Be a detached and passive observer and simply feel your most basic and fundamental being. This inherently immense being has been respectfully called 'the ground of being'

J. Krishnamurti used the term "choiceless awareness" to describe his meditation method. This means being conscious without the thought process choosing something smaller than your vast fundamental being to focus on. Consciousness is like a glass ball floating in the depth of space. Light and sensory input flows into the field of consciousness from all directions. When you think, you focus your attention on just one area of sensory input or you create a thought from memory stored within the brain. With 'choiceless awareness' you are not thinking and not remembering: just floating and letting sensory input flow through you from all directions without manipulating that input with the thought process. You live in the moment and become totally open. This openness attracts energy from all sides of the universe which pushes you even higher.

Another method is to lend special awareness to the breathing process felt in the belly. Just behind and below your navel (belly button) lies the hara. The hara is a natural balancing point of your consciousness that can be thought of as the centre of your subtle body. No one really knows what the hara actually is but we can use it to our advantage. When your consciousness is centred at the hara instead of in the head your thinking process slows down and can even stop. When the thinking process slows down you can relax in the expanded world of pure being. Trying to stop distracting thoughts by will power alone can often lead to even more thoughts and a self-defeating inner struggle. By transferring your centre of consciousness to the hara thoughts gradually disappear on their own without any inner conflict. This is why you see Buddha statues with a big belly. This is an esoteric message that the hara is a key to meditation.

Sit quietly and focus on your belly as it moves in and out as you breathe. Over time the hara point will become noticeable as your meditation grows stronger. We all feel the hara when startled or in intense danger. Sudden emergencies, such as near collisions on the highway, tend to activate the hara centre. You get a 'gut reaction' from sudden danger. You can nourish the feeling of the hara by simply paying passive attention to it. This relaxed concentration is very close to doing nothing yet it is still a subtle effort. Drinking warm liquids such as herb tea or a cup of hot water before meditation sessions relaxes the gut and facilitates awareness of the hara. Overeating and consuming cold drinks tends to make hara awareness more difficult.

The use of meaningful incantations, described in detail in the next section, is quite different from mantra use and can help bring consciousness to a razor sharp clarity. For example repeating the words 'I am the space...I have always been the space.' for a period of up to one minute can be very helpful in focusing the consciousness on the infinite. Do it much longer and the words start to lose their meaning and the exercise degrades into a mantra, defeating the purpose of increasing wakefulness.

Mantras have proven to be medically helpful for some because they can unleash hormones that temporarily calm the mind. Mantras are healthier than taking tranquilizers but are fundamentally different from meditation which relies on the purifying fire of self-observation. Self-observation is a difficult task that requires courage and an endurance of character and spirit.

Real meditation has the real payoff of leading to a naturally calm expanded state of consciousness, not just an artificially silenced mind that remains fundamentally shallow.

A Self-inquiry Incantation

There are powerful words that can help your meditation but they form a strategic questioning, not a mantra. Ramana Maharshi was a beloved Indian teacher who reached enlightenment through self-inquiry, by asking the most fundamental question "Who am I?" Here is a self-inquiry technique that expands Ramana Maharshi's method to make it even more powerful. Speak out loud the following incantation with total intensity before and/or during formal sitting meditation sessions. By the term "total intensity" I mean the same level of intensity you would feel if you were just told that you had only one hour left to live. Be emotional, use your hands and body language if it helps. Plead with the universe the following question.

What is this ball of consciousness?...What is this ball of consciousness?...What is this ball of consciousness? - *You can repeat this question up to a dozen times if the spirit moves you.*

I am not this!...I am not this!...I am not this!

I have always been the space...I have always been the space...I have always been the space. - *You can repeat this statement up to a dozen times.*

I cut these bonds of attachment **now**!

Do these words sound silly? Laughter is good for meditation and the words are humorous but the method itself is deeply serious in the sense that it works, often with startling, electrically shocking power. You invoke this questioning incantation from the hara centre, not from the head. Resonate the words deep inside you without thinking of intellectual explanations of who you are.

Over time you will find the words become a trigger mechanism which allows you to instantly drop all peripheral involvement and come home to your true cosmic being. We all have the same essential being and that being is cosmic. No one is left out of this universe. If you are a part of the universe you are all of the universe! The small 'I' is dropped and only the big 'I' remains. Then you can have a good belly laugh and that is the way to end most of your own meditation sessions. Meditate until you start laughing from the hara centre.

The statement 'I am not this!' means that you are not just the temporary world of illusion that Hindus call **maya**, the ever changing peripheral world of transient events. You are the **changeless being** beyond the realm of the senses. Your identity extends far beyond birth and death and beyond simple pleasure and pain. You are the infinite void from which all is born. That is the meaning of the statement 'I have always been the space'. Nothing is bigger than space and space contains all that exists.

When speaking the words 'I cut these bonds of attachment **now**!' it helps to slap the back of the right hand against the palm of the left hand upon saying the word '**now**!' Reverse hands if you are left handed. This creates a loud cracking sound which adds drama and helps wake up the central nervous system. You can use this questioning technique only at the beginning of formal sitting meditation sessions or you can repeat the incantation every five to ten minutes during the session to help keep yourself focused. Combining this self-inquiry incantation with the mirror gazing technique described below creates a **super method** of great power and intensity.

Word exercises are not for all students of meditation. If you try them and feel nothing then concentrate on other methods first. As you slowly change your methods will change with you. A method that is unusable now may be of great help to you in the future.

Mirror Gazing

Some students find that the use of a mirror virtually doubles the power of their meditation sessions. Sit in front of a mirror and gaze into your own eyes for at least twenty minutes, allowing the eyes to deeply relax their focus. Alternative methods are to gaze just above your head at the reflection of the wall behind you or to focus your eyes on the reflected image of your own forehead (stimulates the Ajna chakra). Become a silent witness to the act of seeing and observing.

The reflected image you see in the mirror may take on strange new forms. Your body may appear to change from one race to another; the same soul in different incarnations. Are the faces you see in the mirror from past lives, fantasies of the mind, or the result of the fluid nature of your visual field consciousness? Do not expect to answer this question with certainty because it is inherently unanswerable. Over time the many faces will disappear and you will consistently see only one face.

Enjoy the mirror gazing and then stand up for two minutes, maintaining your heightened awareness as you change position. Then resume sitting in quiet meditation for ten minutes with eyes almost totally closed, allowing in just two slits of light. Be aware of your being existing in its most basic form without activity. Combining this mirror gazing technique with the self-inquiry incantation previously detailed can increase its effectiveness tremendously, creating a **super method**.

Eye Gazing

To do this technique you must have a partner of the opposite sex, preferably someone you love. It is identical to the mirror gazing technique described above except you look into the eyes of your loved one. Sit together staring softly into your partner's eyes for twenty minutes, then stand for two minutes, then sit in quiet meditation with eyes almost totally closed for ten minutes. This technique can readily lead to romantic intimacy so pick your partner carefully.

Cathartic Dancing Meditation

Cathartic Dancing Meditation is a cosmic powerhouse that can be used by students in good health with a normal cardiovascular system. As it is a physically strenuous exercise, one should get a complete physical examination by a competent doctor before experimenting with this technique. Explain the method to your doctor and ask if it would be physically dangerous for you to do. He won't understand your motives for wanting to do it but he can tell you if he thinks your body and heart can safely handle it. As with jogging or mountain climbing you must practise this method at your own risk.

Cathartic Dancing Meditation is similar to Rajneesh Dynamic Meditation but is simpler, easier to do, and is more likely to keep you interested month after month, year after year. Neither method is really new as Sufis, Druids, and countless other esoteric and tribal cultures have used similar techniques for centuries. Most students will benefit from doing Cathartic Dancing Meditation daily for a period of between one and five years. After five years it has usually done its job and the student can move on to more subtle methods.

Cathartic Dancing Meditation changes you from head to toe and benefits all the other meditation techniques you may practise. It also helps develop a powerful hara centre. Cathartic Dancing Meditation has three stages and lasts for forty minutes.

Stage 1 (ten minutes) Start by standing with your eyes closed and breath deep and fast through your nose continuously. If you are only physically capable of doing deep breathing for five minutes then reduce the length of the first stage without feeling guilty. Remember that you are doing this method to help your meditation, not to physically injure yourself. Allow your body to move freely as you breathe. You can jump up and down, sway back and forth, or use any physical motion that helps you pump more oxygen into your lungs.

Stage 2 (twenty minutes) The second stage is a celebration of catharsis and wild and spontaneous dancing. Let go totally and act as an ancient human being dancing in tribal celebration. Energetic, nonverbal background music is highly recommended. African tribal drum music works especially well. You may roll on the ground and do strange spontaneous body movements. Allow the body to move within the limits of not hurting yourself or others. For once in your life screaming is encouraged. You must act out any anger you have in a safe way such as beating the earth with your hands. All the suppressed emotions from your subconscious mind are to be released. If at anytime during the second stage you feel that your energy level is starting to decline you can resume deep and fast breathing to give yourself a boost.

Stage 3 (ten minutes) This stage is complete relaxation and quite. Flop down on your back, get comfortable, and just let go. Be as if a dead man totally surrendered to the cosmos. Enjoy the tremendous energy you have unleashed in the first two stages and be a silent witness to it. Observe the feeling of the ocean flowing into the drop. Become the ocean.

This spontaneous dancing meditation technique is intended to grow with the student and change as the student changes. After a few years of vigorously practising this method the first two stages of the meditation may drop away spontaneously. You may then begin the meditation by taking a few deep breaths and immediately go deep into the ecstasy of the third stage. If practised correctly this method is health giving and fun.

WARNING: Obviously one must practice Cathartic Dancing Meditation in a safe location and not near the edge of a cliff or on a hard surface where one might fall and break one's skull. A large room or hall with thick carpeting is good. Outdoors in the early morning on a soft and well tended lawn with group participation is best. Do it on an empty stomach and avoid falling into dangerous objects such as windows. It is allowable to briefly open one's eyes occasionally to maintain your location. Create a safety zone around your dancing and spontaneous body movements. Be courteous to neighbors and delete the screaming if it will be heard by others.

Almost all Westernised Indians are head oriented and emotionally repressed. For them a chaotic, spontaneous, and emotionally cleansing technique like Cathartic Dancing Meditation is vital for serious progress to be made quickly. The physical benefits of this technique obviate any need for hatha yoga or traditional kundalini yoga methods. Cathartic Dancing Meditation is so multidimensional in its effects and benefits that it deserves the designation of a **super method**.

Soul Awareness

This method is recommended for those students who have practised the other described techniques long enough to gain a feeling of floating bodilessness. If you cannot feel your subtle body you cannot practise this method effectively. In the beginning it should only be used during formal sitting meditation sessions. Latter on, after you have gained some progress with this method, you can use an evolved version of the meditation while engaged in any activity that does not require thinking or your full attention. For example you can practice it while walking in a safe location away from highway traffic.

Begin this method by sitting with eyes fully open. Softly gaze at a blank wall or, more preferably, look out a window at a distant vista. With the mind's eye (the eye of consciousness behind your body's purely physical eyes) define your field of visual consciousness as a circle. Imagine the top of your field of consciousness as the 12 o'clock position on a clock and the bottom of your field of consciousness as the 6 o'clock position. With your mind's eye, not your physical eyes, slowly sweep your attention clockwise from the top 12 o'clock position down to the 6 o'clock position, then on to the 9 o'clock position and then back up to the 12 o'clock position. Repeat this process in the counterclockwise direction. Mentally strain to observe the very outer edges of your visual field of consciousness where the light of consciousness turns into the darkness of empty space. Go on repeating this process until you feel you have had enough.

This is a soul awareness exercise, not an eye exam, and that is why it is recommended only for students with a number of years of experience in meditation. After practising this method for some time one can begin to transform the method into one of sudden expansion of awareness. You can gain the ability to perceive the complete 360 degrees of the outer edges of your consciousness in one jump. This feels like stepping back, literally out of your own mind, and looking back into your mind from a close and friendly distance. You become identified with the void and space around the flame of consciousness and this makes the flame grow even brighter. This truly esoteric method is difficult to fully explain and there are aspects of it that you will have to learn on your own through practice.

One discovers from this technique that our visual field of consciousness is roughly American football shaped with greater width than height. This is because our brains evolved out of a need to look for food and danger more on the horizontal axis than on the vertically axis. To survive you need to be aware of what is on your right and left more than what is directly below your feet or above your head. This soul awareness method has a deprogramming effect that allows one to appreciate the play of existence as an ever changing drama. You feel as if you are in it but also out of it and beyond it. **Combining the advanced form of this soul awareness method with the self-inquiry incantation described earlier creates a powerful super method.**

Sweeping House

This is an easy technique designed to quickly sweep the clutter of thoughts from your mind. It can be used before starting formal sitting meditation sessions or anytime during the day you feel you have lost your existential focus. Begin by placing both hands behind your head with fingers interlocked. Rest your hands at the point where the neck and the head meet. Then slowly sweep your hands over the top of your head. Imagine that your hands are gathering up all your thoughts as they move. When your hands reach your forehead use a flicking motion as you simultaneously unlock your fingers and throw your hands away from your face. Feel as if all your thoughts are being swept out of your head and discarded. Do this between three and seven times as needed and then relax and enjoy the inner silence. This method takes less than one minute to do and can be used at bedtime to help free the mind from the problems of the day.

You can be Creative

After you have become comfortable with the meditation techniques individually you can learn to incorporate them simultaneously to multiply their effectiveness. For example, combining mirror gazing, hara awareness, the soul awareness technique, and the use of the self-inquiry incantation can be extremely powerful. That combined **super method** is currently my own favourite technique but I do not believe it can be done successfully without first practising the methods separately for a considerable period of time.

There are no rigid 'one size fits all' meditation techniques. Follow your intuition and let the methods evolve to fit your own individuality. Don't take the time suggestions for methods as rigid limits. If you feel you want to extend your meditation sessions to more than an hour then do so. What I have written here are just general guidelines to get people started on the path. Let your hair flow free and go with the flow and the ecstasy.

How Long Should I Meditate?

The time a person needs to spend in formal meditation sessions to gain maximum benefit depends on ever-changing individual circumstances. If you are meditating with a group you will gain from the group energy and go farther with less effort. If you are fortunate enough to be living close to an enlightened teacher you may be able to absorb some of his high energy without any effort at all. If you are meditating alone, without support from others, then you will have to do all the heavy lifting yourself.

My general recommendation is that 1 hour a day spent in formal meditation sessions is a minimal effort. Meditation only works for those who are hungry for it and if you cannot spare that small amount of time for meditation then you will probably not gain substantial results. Most people will be helped significantly by meditating 1 hour a day but progress may be so slow that you barely feel it. If you wish to go faster, so that you can feel the wind in your hair with clearly recognizable progress, then I suggest 1.5 to 2.5 hours a day.

Two 45 minute sessions, one in the morning and one in the evening, works well for most people. Adding a third 45 minute session in the afternoon is stronger medicine if you can manage it. Spending more time than that in formal meditation sessions becomes difficult for most people as it takes you away from family, friends, job, and social responsibilities. If you are single, of independent means, and naturally reclusive then you may spend as much time in formal meditation sessions as you wish.

A specific recommendation for young, physically fit beginners would be to practise Cathartic Dancing Meditation in the morning and the mirror gazing-self-inquiry incantation super method at night. That powerhouse combination will produce owl eyed Zen wakefulness very rapidly and the combination represents a complete meditation system. It is of paramount importance to practise mindfulness throughout the day. To be of any real value meditation must become a full-time way of living rather than a strictly segregated activity.

How Long does it Take to Become Enlightened?

Meditation is a pleasure in itself and the healthiest approach is to enjoy the journey without thoughts of gaining a pot of gold at the end of some distant rainbow. Ask yourself who or what will reach that imagined goal? If our petty little minds reach enlightenment will we be enlightened at all? Thinking about goals takes us further away from choiceless awareness, relaxation, and ecstasy and is thus counterproductive. It is best to fully enjoy the journey of meditation without seeking any title, credentials, or an ultimate brass ring that we can selfishly own and boast about to others.

Things to do, things to avoid, and things to consider

Work in groups when possible as group energy can multiply the energy of an individual many times over.

Remember that meditation is an escape to reality, not an escape from reality. Avoid any guru or group that asks you to deny truth.

Don't limit yourself to just one teacher. The single guru approach can lead to 'cult thinking' with its small mindedness and 'us vs. them' syndrome.

Avoid fads and complicated philosophies that give your mind more to think about. Meditation is a step beyond the thought process. No philosophy can adequately describe man's place in the universe. Concentrate on meditation in this moment and not on ancient scriptures.

Take good care of your health. Get a proper diet without becoming a food fanatic. A vegetarian diet supplemented with dairy products is generally best. Eggs are not harmful to meditation and if you wish to eat meat then fish is a better choice than foul or mutton. If you have a medical problem like hypoglycemia you may have to eat meat just to survive. A vegetarian or semi-vegetarian diet is usually best for students of meditation but food should not be made the fundamental basis of your practice. Remember that Adolf Hitler was a perfect vegetarian yet his diet did not save his soul or even make him nonviolent.

Avoid drugs and alcohol. Drugs are not an effective path to enlightenment but they are a quick path to misery and insanity.

Have sex when you wish and do not force celibacy upon yourself in the hopes it will lead to enlightenment. To meditate one must be in a very natural and relaxed state of mind without repression or tension. Celibacy can only be of value if it occurs spontaneously without effort or thought. The majority of famous Eastern gurus who have proclaimed celibacy publicly have practised intercourse privately. Why make sex a big secret and why have two faces? Many fully enlightened humans have had sexual relations even after enlightenment. There is no relationship between abstinence and spirituality.

Do practise 'choiceless awareness' throughout the day. Meditation must become as continuous and spontaneous as breathing.

Don't make meditation a competition and drop any hidden agenda you may have to use it to control others. Legitimate motives for meditation are the desire for tranquillity and ecstasy, freedom from suffering, and the pure adventure of self-exploration.

Don't turn your meditation into a business. People who make a profit from intercourse have turned something beautiful into something ugly. Those who make money from meditation have transformed a noble path into a sordid back alley. Whether you are a sexual prostitute or a spiritual prostitute the fundamental quality of your mind is the same.

Be completely honest and have just one face, not two.

For every action there is a reaction, not just in theoretical physics but in ordinary human life as well. When you create positive actions you will eventually reap positive reactions for yourself and for others. In this way what we call ethics and morality are woven into the very fabric of the universe right down to the subatomic level.

Enlightenment

The fastest meditation method is to live in the company of an enlightened human being. Enlightened teachers can expand your consciousness without the slightest effort on your part. All you need to do is to be open to the spontaneous transfer of energy. Fully enlightened human beings are very rare.

When it comes to teachers, even fully enlightened teachers, **take the best and leave the rest.** No human being has ever been perfect and without major flaws and limitations. Only myths can give the illusion of perfection and that is why most of society continues to worship invented myths rather than accepting reality as it is, warts and all. Enlightened humans are vastly expanded human beings, not perfect human beings.

The traditional guru-disciple relationship is now passé and inappropriate for modern students of meditation. Be a devoted disciple but make your ultimate guru **the all and the everything**, the ultimate truth of the total cosmic existence. Use teachers as temporary tools on your path to self-realization but do not allow yourself to become the captive servant of one fallible human mind.

■ ■ ■

13

JAMES VAN PRAAGH

SPIRITUAL HEALING

James Van Praagh is renowned for conveying messages between realms. He is the best-selling author of three books: Talking to Heaven, Reaching to Heaven and Healing Grief. He travels the world spreading the knowledge of life after death by lecturing, giving demonstrations and conducting spiritual tours.

Many spiritual traditions say that the source of all disease, as well as the source of all healing, is spiritual in nature. James Van Praagh also believes that all things are spirit and are derived from spirit. When you look at life from that perspective, he says, it takes on a whole new meaning. So, when you question anything, first you have to begin with the core, which is your spiritual self, whether that's disease, fear, or abundance.

For most people the individual spirit is a person's soul and the larger spirit, the Holy Spirit, is the spirit of God. For Van Praagh It's a matter of semantics. "I think it's all. I think that God is imbued in all of us and God is spirit. I don't think we should get caught up in the semantics of it. I also think that we need to realize that there are different parts, different aspects of who we are. There are many big parts of ourselves, many bodies, if you will, of humankind. Higher selves, soul selves, ego selves, different bodies of man."

Those are involved also, but the Spirit of God is in all of those bodies, too, the common thread in all.

In terms of the seven chakras or seven centers in the body, they are linked with the seven levels or planes, and each corresponds with the body. Each centre corresponds to various colours or modes of sound, called harmonics. They are different levels of being within each centre.

It goes back to having a relationship with our spiritual selves, which is knowing who you are. With deep meditation, you are having a relationship with the inner part of you instead of the outer part of you. So much of society in our world is caught up with the outside, and what you see in the physical, and disregarding what's on the inside. All things start from within. All things start with thought and creativity. We are the ones who are really responsible for creating our world, based upon our thoughts. So once people get into silence and have a relationship with themselves from the inner side of their being, they begin to see things in a much clearer perspective. Choices can be made much easier, when you are sitting in a position of balance and peacefulness in the heart rather than just the head, from truth rather than from fear.

The more you meditate, the more you are able to create choices, it comes from the right perspective and will bring about the change that you want. All of life is balance, and that includes health concerns. Disease is not being in balance, not being in harmony with oneself, not being true to oneself, not being in harmony with who you are. Therefore, if you are balanced, it helps defeat disease.

Many people have unrealistic expectations about life. What this means in terms of spiritual health is that instead of making life happen, we can easily get caught up in "victim consciousness." Many of us find it much easier to say "Poor, pitiful me. How can these things happen to me?" We blame others for our problems and don't take responsibility. This is true not only of spiritual health, but of many experiences in life. Even in many religions, people are encouraged to give the responsibility to God or to Jesus or whatever, instead of taking responsibility themselves. We have to learn to take responsibility for our lives and our choices, and that comes as a very hard lesson for some people. Everyone is here to learn lessons in life, at their own rate, according to Van Praagh. This is our schoolroom. There are some lessons that are much more difficult than others. It's up to the individual. Again, it comes down to choices. Are you going to use the situation to better yourself, to learn, to evolve? Or are you going to use it to hold back, to be a victim? It is up to you to make that decision.

It does seem that if people are happy with themselves and what they are doing with their life, then they are less likely to be ill. People need to be honest, but some people are very critical of themselves. It comes down to love, as everything does. You have to love yourself enough to know yourself. Many diseases and sickness come out of negative thought, imbalances, impurity. If we are to be true to ourselves, come from a place of truth and of real love of ourselves, then we will be generating loving thoughts, creative thoughts, and thoughts of balance, peace and health.

One of the things that Van Praagh has talked about in his books is that when people cross over to the other side, there is an earth-like heaven where we have youthful bodies. That is what he calls the astral level.

The astral level is an exact replica or counterpart of the physical world. So you have a body that is very much like the physical one, only a pure body. The astral world is almost like a temporary cross over station which has houses and trees and gardens and so forth, which appear very solid and very real. "I talk a lot about this in my book Reaching to Heaven. This astral world is really there to help the individual to realize that they are no longer part of the physical world, yet they are still alive. This way it is not as shocking to them when they go and it seems like a very real world. This is my understanding, but of course I don't know anything for sure until I pass over myself. This is what a spirit has told me."

The astral plane is like a waiting room in between incarnations. Although there are other levels too, that we go to. So once we've become adapted to ourselves in spirit form, then perhaps we go to a higher level in the astral. We could say it's an in-between, and of course we can stay there as long as we need to because there is no such thing as time in spirit. We can't measure by years or months, or whatever, because it doesn't work over there like that. There are no clocks. So we stay there until another situation is set up on the earth level. Then we come back to work out karmic obligations or to go through various lessons. You have to remember that the earth isn't the only place to learn lessons; there are other universes and other places of life. The earth is one of the places that there is free will. Most lessons on earth have to do with love.

Ultimately, the highest level is the clear white light or the Buddhic or God conscious plane. "Godhead...purity of love. I think love is the thing. Once we get to the realization of loving ourselves and breathing that love into every single experience of every single day then you start to make a big progression at that point. But we also have to be mindful of the fact that we have a physical body and that we are on a physical earth right now. We are spirit encased in a physical body. We have to be feed ourselves spiritually every day, of course, but we also have to be mindful of our physical bodies. We have to exercise, we have to eat right, sleep, rest, we have to treat our body as if it is a temple of God. So many of us don't. I find that when spirits come through, many times they talk about how they didn't take care of themselves. That they weren't that health conscious or aware of themselves, and they should have been. They regret that they didn't pay more attention to their physical bodies as far as health and diet. I do believe that there are some people that come back to this earth to really learn about being in a physical body."

We can focus more spiritually if our bodies and mind are aligned, because, according to Van Praagh in the readings that he does, he does a scan of the body, he will actually see the force, the prana energy going up and down the spine. He can see where it's blocked at certain parts of the spine. He will say to that person, "You have trouble in your back here, you have trouble in your neck here, you have trouble in your stomach here." And they will say "Yes!" He sees the blockage of that energy. He sees it on an energetic level before it is descended into the physical level.

We are celebrating our daily life in the body we were given by taking care of it and remembering these positive, united spiritual thoughts. It seems that when we are old and on our death bed, that we should have the same goal in mind remembering God and that would create the highest death, leaving on the out breath and visualizing the light. If we have that awareness of our God selves or awareness of spirit, it certainly will help with the transition. Death is a natural transition of life. It is so natural, and so many of us don't know about it. Until we go through it, we are fearful of it. It's a very natural state of being and in many ways, we do this every night when we go to sleep and leave the physical body. When it's the time of death when the silver cord is severed, we know on a conscious level that we are leaving the body. It's a very natural thing, and many spirits will say it was painless, it was no big deal, it was very natural.

We can avoid a lot of the pain while we are alive and in the transition by being aligned with spiritual thoughts, but if people fear physical death for themselves and their loved ones, then it makes the transition much harder. It seems like if people think this life is the be-all-end-all that is where all the fear comes from. With fear, it seems that it is harder leading up to the transition. One may go through a lot of pain, and it's unfortunate because you don't have to do that. The fear unfortunately makes you think death is going to be horrible and it is going to be painful, and it isn't.

Fear seems to make it longer for the transition to take place. The transition is going to happen in God's time rather than our time. It's going to happen when it's meant to happen. It would make the transition much easier if there is no fear involved. "For myself, I am fearful of the type of death I would have. I would not want it to be a painful type of death, nor would anyone. Everyone would like to die in a quick manner. I think that many times the type of death we have is karmic. The most important thing to realize is that the soul cannot be harmed, and that death itself is not painful."

If your mind is on the soul carrying on, and you are in a spiritual place, then whether or not you see it coming (like if a car hits you that you don't even see), if you are in a spiritual mode, then you are ready for the transition any time. For example Yogananda, who was ready for his death, got everyone in a room and said something like "Okay, I am going to be leaving now." And he left his body and that was it. That is possible to do.

What happens when people are very ill (with something like cancer or AIDS or a disease that really debilitates the body over a long period of time), is that several months before the actual death the silver cord connected to the solar plexus chakra begins to wear down to different levels, like a peeling off. The person that is passing over will go in and out of the body on a conscious level, almost like a dress rehearsal, and will become aware of leaving the body. They are aware that they are outside of the body, and then when it's time that the silver cord is finally severed, they are okay, they are used to it, and it goes very naturally for them. This happens quite often.

What Van Praagh calls physical seed atom is the core essence of who you are at the spirit level of being. Recorded in this atom is every single experience that you have ever had. Here's an interesting analogy. Right now I am planting bulbs in the ground. At the bottom of the bulb there are roots. Out of that root, then the bulb, comes a flower. So where the roots are, it is like the seed atom. Through your lifetimes experiences are recorded there and you grow and grow and grow, and you flourish. That is the root of who you are, the seed of who you are.

So when you pass over to the other side and you are in that astral state, which is linked with the physical plane, there must be some residual seed atom there from which you develop the next body later on.

It's almost as if the karma is information that is stored like on a zip disk. When you move into your next life, this karmic information is downloaded through the life cord into the seed atom. Thus we have a link, habits and patterns, even diseases, left over from the past lifetime out of karma.

The soul will come back when the soul needs to come back. "I have found through research that I have done, that a soul that was in a person that died as a child, and in some suicide cases, the soul tends to come back faster and won't be long in the other world. From what I understand, we come back in "soul groups." Those souls in the group like to come back when the time is right for all of them. Not only are you as an individual evolving, but you are connected to a soul group that is evolving together as well, so as one develops, you all develop. Then you move on together."

What if you are waiting to be reunited with a loved one but they have already reincarnated as someone else? "I tell people not to worry about this; you will always be with that person on one level or another. You are thinking of it from a physical, linear point of view. This is just this one personality you remember from the earth. But the soul is so much bigger, grander than that. You will recognize that soul when you pass over because there's a part that remains in the spirit realm. There are ways of existence that we are not aware of in the physical body; we are limited here."

There are certain souls that go through many incarnations together, and travel in soul groups. And relationships vary from one incarnation to the next, depending on what you have to learn from each other. So our relationship with others impacts our individual health because we are learning to share and care beyond ourselves. Look at it as a ripple in the water; you throw pebbles in the water and you have little waves that branch out. What you create with your thought you are sending out the same way. So if you think ill health, and if you think disease, you will create that. Also, if you have negative thinking towards others it ripples out. We are all connected. What goes around comes around. That will come back to you, although it won't come back the way you think it will.

"Part of my work is not only to make people aware that they are spirit, but to let them know that the spirit is eternal. You cannot kill spirit, you cannot kill energy. I hope that part of my work is to illuminate people and I have seen it happen. When you open yourself up to this awareness that you are spirit, you then not only know that you are eternal, but that you can create the world you want. Once you become aware that you are God, that you are the creative force within you, and that you can create everything; whether it is health, abundance, happiness, love; you have what's in you to do that. This is where I get so much out of my work, to open people up to that so that we change lives. We are not living in a limited point of view; we are now living in a limitless perspective."

So why would one chose to incarnate as an evil entity, such as a serial killer? "I don't think one is choosing that, per se. I think there might be aspects to a personality which need to learn and evolve and grow and I think that soul might have put themselves in a situation where they could learn from it; or perhaps not learn this time. They might not make the right choice because of some past incarnations or some behavioral trait. Like unfulfilled karma, prior lifetimes...They might go into the same pattern again. Every single soul is evolving, and that is why we are here. Some will evolve faster than others. In the case of a serial killer, it might be very much about lower animal instincts of their personality that have not evolved yet."

When we are in spirit, in that so-called waiting room between physical lives, we have full memory of our past lives so that we can learn from our karma. When you pass into spirit, you have an awareness of all of the lives that you've lived, and all the experiences. You see all the good and bad that you have done. From this you set up new karma, or new situations to work out in another lifetime. But while we are on this earth level, we go through what is called the "Valley of Forgetfulness" where those lifetimes are cut off from us on our conscious level.

There are a lot of stories about people having a close brush with death but then surviving, and you often hear the phrase, "It wasn't his time to go." That is probably because we have a preset amount of time for each incarnation. Before we come back there is a blueprint, and in the blueprint are the various experiences that we set out to learn in this lifetime. There is a time when the spirit is done with those lessons and it's time to go back home. That is probably predestined, and also the type of death is predestined. But our free will is probably involved as well. Or someone else's free will becomes involved in our termination. For example, if someone robs you and shoots you, then you are dead, you are gone. That might not have been the time you were set to go, because that person's free will was involved in your path. This type of thing can happen as well.

In Van Praagh's first book, Talking to Heaven, the main focus was on communicating with loved ones who have already passed on. With his second book, Reaching to Heaven, his goal was to guide us to rediscovering our own inner link. In his latest book, Healing Grief, Van Praagh focuses completely on the subject of grieving. He says he wrote Healing Grief because there were thousands and thousands of people from around the world who got stuck in grief. It seemed to be quite an obstacle. They didn't know what to do with their lives or how to move on. He want to give them a way out; a key to a doorway to help them out and away from the obstacles. "I want people to learn how to live with grief and to not let that hold them back in life. Instead, people can learn to use the grief to help make them stronger, and as an opportunity for growth."

In the book Van Praagh talks about moving through anger and denial, toward acceptance. There are many stages of grief, he says. The most important thing to realize is that people will grieve differently at different times and in different ways. There is not just one set way to grieve. Not one right way, not one wrong way. Each situation is unique to that individual. So we cannot apply our own laws and rules upon someone else's grief.

One of most significant aspects of your work is that it does allow people to learn to let go and move on with their lives.

"For spiritual healing I would say the number one thing is to get involved with meditation, and go into the silence. Work on the energetic level as well; learn how to balance your energy levels by paying attention to the nuances around you. We need to pay attention to the spiritual signs and symbols and signals around us, because we have them every single day. Learn to listen to them. Learn to see them, not from just a physical point of view but from a spiritual point of view. Be aware, be mindful. That is the number one path toward spiritual healing."

■ ■ ■

14

JOHN McDOUGALL

ORGANIC HEALING

Dr. John McDougall is an educator and best-selling author. He is the founder and director of the McDougall Programme at St. Helena Hospital in Napa, California. He lectures nationally, and has appeared regularly on television and radio. He is the author of many books, including The McDougall Programme: Twelve Days to Dynamic Health and his most recent book, The McDougall Programme for Women.

Dr. MacDougall has been campaigning keep the environment as clean as possible and showing that environmental chemicals that are causing cancers and also diseases as serious as Parkinson's disease. "I ask people to leave out foods that are high on the food chain. Ninety percent of our dioxin intake, which causes cancer and other serious problems, comes from eating dairy. This applies to other environmental chemicals as well. So if you cut out the dairy and meat, you've really cut down on your risk. But if you want to eat meat in small amounts on occasion, you can still enjoy good health. There are also brands now that are made from animals raised with more natural lifestyles and feeds, but you're still dealing with rich foods. You're dealing with high fat, high protein, low carbohydrate, low fiber, and if that's the centerpiece of your diet, which it is for most Americans — I don't care how organic it is — you're still going to have a high likelihood of heart disease, obesity and diabetes. These foods are just too rich. The problem with people in America is they like to eat like kings and queens. They eat the richest diet ever known, and as a result they look like kings and queens. The solution to the problem is to make feasts special again; have rich foods only on special occasions. It's the answer to health problems individually and also nationally.

He also avoids bio-engineered foods, both in his personal diet and company, Dr. McDougall's Right Foods, which has no genetically engineered foods in the products. "Because it just didn't sound right. Research is preliminary and there's arguments on both sides."

"The McDougall Programme for Women" came out because in addition to being interested in the dietary practices of people, he is a medical doctor and through the years he has been really concerned about misinformation given to patients. A lot of his writings have been about misinformation in terms of bypass surgery and other types of operations. "I went into medicine with the idea that I was going to save all these lives with all the tricks and tools that medical doctors learn. And what I found was that very few of my patients got well. That I often did harm to them. This was quite disturbing to me as a young doctor. But what was even more disturbing to me was to find out that this failure had been fairly well documented in the scientific literature. Now that literature sits on the library shelf, because it doesn't fit into anybody's advertising campaign. What I've done through the years, in addition to teaching good health habits and good diet to people, is to try to protect them from the medical business by informing them of things that are wrong. Science says one thing and the public believes another because the public relations machine benefits the economics of the drug industry and the medical industry. Anyway, the book talks about the basic issues of health and disease in women. Chemical estrogens in rich foods cause the early onset of sexual maturity in girls. Breast cancer is an environmental disease that has to do with the fats and synthetic chemicals in your diet and also the lack of plant chemicals in your diet to protect you. Mammography is a fraud."

The January 8, 2000 issue of The Lancet carried an article stating that mammography is unjustifiable. Actually, of the eight studies done, six of them show that it doesn't work — and yet the American public believes that this is a time honored, definite way of saving their lives from breast cancer. There's also a chapter in the book on natural treatment of breast cancer. "I published the first study in the 1980's on treating breast cancer with a healthy diet. I was considered a radical then, but there have been many studies in major journals since then that say once you get breast cancer if you change your diet you will live much longer", he says.

Menopause comes later with the rich American diet compared to a healthy diet. This is due to the over stimulation of the body with estrogen over a prolonged period of time, from factory farmed animals which are brought to maturity faster with artificial growth hormones.

The cause of osteoporosis, also, is primarily diet, McDougall stresses. With all of the red meat and poultry, seafood, cheese and eggs, the rich American diet is a very acidic diet. That acid has to be buffered when you eat it. So the bones dissolve and then changes take place in the kidneys that cause the body to urinate the bones through the kidney system out into the toilet. Sometimes bones resolidify and they form calcium kidney stones. So we should eat more alkaline foods, to balance the acid/alkaline ratio in our bodies. Eat fruits and vegetables to adjust the body's pH towards greater alkalinity.

That is more proof for a more vegetable-centered diet. That's what almost every scientist in the world is saying. That you should eat more plants, and less animal products, and less processed foods. Eggs fall into the same category as other animal products. They are very acidic, very high cholesterol, no carbohydrates, no fiber. The book ends with a whole section of recipes for a healthy diet. He started his natural foods line. They are in 4,000 stores now. They are 16 products now. Cereals, soups and dinners. They all have natural ingredients, as organic as possible. They're very low fat and high fiber, no cholesterol. They're tasty and they're selling well.

The whole idea is to make healthy foods available, as well as educating with the books; to make it so simple that people can't say no. If people have excuses like "it doesn't taste good" or "I don't have time," with our products those excuses are gone.

For the last 14 years, Dr. McDougall been running the live-in centre at St. Helena Hospital. People come from around the country and live at the hospital for 12 days. But it doesn't look like a hospital because it's beautifully decorated and such a nice setting. His first book is based on that programme and tells you how to do it at home.

Dr. McDougall thinks it's very important that people realize that they can regain lost health. A lot of folks out there think they're trapped; being fat, sick and dependent on drugs — that's not the case. Well over 80% can get off their medication. Essentially all of them can get their weight down, and get to feeling and functioning well again by doing something cost-free: by eating the right kinds of foods. Actually, you can cut your food bill up to 40% by cutting out animal products and processed foods. Add some exercise and clean up your habits and you will get far greater results than any pill could ever give you. If everyone knew they had that option, he says, he would be the happiest doctor in the world. ■ ■ ■

15

JOHN UPLEDGER

HEALING THROUGH CRANIOSACRAL THERAPY

Dr. John Upledger, D.O., O.M.M., is the creator of two innovative forms of bodywork, CranioSacral Therapy and SomatoEmotional Release. He is a respected educator and author of the excellent and informative book Your Inner Physician and You. He is an Osteopathic Physician, Clinical Reseacher.

CranioSacral Therapy is a very soft touch, hands-on method of treatment. It deals with what he has termed the craniosacral system which is composed of a membrane that is waterproof that encases the brain and spinal cord and carries within it cerebrospinal fluid. The pressure and volume of the fluid go up and down. That makes it a hydraulic system, which needs to be free to move all the time because the fluid should be moving and bringing nutrients to all the neurons and taking away wastes and so forth. With CranioSacral Therapy, we have several entrees into this system — most of them through bony attachments or through direction of energy or pulling of fascia —for alleviating any restrictions that might have accumulated due to injuries or illnesses. This therapy improves the health of the brain and spinal cord, which in turn, affects the whole body.

The membrane has three layers. The outer layer is called the dura mater and it's the waterproof one. It's kind of tough. It has some elasticity, but not a lot. The middle layer is called the arachnoid membrane and it carries a lot of blood vessels. It interacts between the external dura mater, the outer layer and the internal layer which is called the pia mater, which is the one that follows all the little dents and nooks and crannies in the brain. You probably have seen pictures of the surface of the brain and the pia mater follows all those little dents into the brain.

They are all inside the cranial wall, all three of them. All three membranes extend from the head down through the spine to the sacrum. Part of what's needed for good health and good movement is the three layers need to be able to move independently of each other. If they were stuck together and couldn't glide, you wouldn't be able to bend side to side or forward and backward because you wouldn't have that play in there.

So if you do some gentle, regular exercise like swimming, Tai Chi or yoga, that would be good to extend flexibility into later life. The more you get these membranes mobilized, the healthier you'll be. And of course, that extends through your whole body, ultimately, via the nervous system.

The innermost membrane, the pia mater, adheres to the spinal cord going down, and the only place it attaches to bone is where the nerve roots of the spinal cord come out laterally or transversely. Then they attach to openings between the vertebrae, but they're not in the spinal canal, they are out there, maybe a half inch or an inch.

The outermost layer sometimes is free and sometimes attached. Inside the skull itself, it divides into two layers. One layer becomes the internal lining of the skull wall. Then there are little fibers that attach the second layer to it. The inner layer of it has much more mobility. The fiber is restricted somewhat, but not a lot. It glides back and forth a little bit. It's because of this attachment to the bones that we can actually use skull bones to move the membranes and put forces in there that create release of certain restrictions or adhesions that may have occurred.

In Your Inner Physician and You, Dr. Upledger claims that bone actually grows out of the membrane when you are in the womb. "When you are an embryo the surface of the skull itself was all membrane and the bones formed within it. When you are born, that is why you have these fontanels, the soft spots. Those bones haven't grown to fill in the soft spots yet. Actually, at the sutures where bones come together, you might have a gap of an eighth of an inch or even a quarter of an inch wide when you are first born. This is because when you are delivered your head has to deform coming through the birth canal. So one of your skull bones will override the other in order to make the head narrower to get through narrow places."

After you're born your head gradually becomes rounder. That's exactly where CranioSacral Therapy could start. Heads are supposed to expand and become rounder and sometimes they don't. They get stuck, and at a time like that, a good therapist can release that stuck place between two bones where it didn't fully expand in the space of a few minutes. You can take away a lifetime of trouble for that child right at that point.

When we are adults, it's commonly thought that those different plates of the skull fuse together, which is a myth that Dr. Upledger explodes in his book. "British anatomy taught that the bones were fused as you became an adult. Italian anatomy did not. I think that is because British anatomy studied embalmed cadavers. They had been sitting in a laboratory, they had been embalmed, and because of post mortem and chemical changes that occurred, these sutures appeared to be calcified. Italian anatomists worked on fresh cadavers, and they could see that there is a lot of elastic tissue, a lot of blood vessels, and a whole lot of things that are there so that the bones can move, one in relationship to the other. I didn't know about this difference (between the British and Italians) until I was lecturing in Israel and I was making a strong point before a bunch of doctors about how this systems works and how these bones are not immovable in adults, they are not fused, and nobody really seemed to be really excited about that. Finally after I tried to reiterate it the second time in different terms, because I thought they didn't understand me, one of the doctors said, "Let me show you something." He pulled out an Italian anatomy book published in 1920. He translated it for me from the Italian, "The bones of the skull do not fuse except under diseased conditions throughout life." So we have that myth in this country because we have studied and drawn our education from British anatomy. We just reinvented the wheel!"

Bone motion needs to continue throughout life, and the slight motion that is there is accommodated, according to Dr. Upledger, because the sutures themselves have elastic and collagen fibers in them so that they allow for some movement (on the order of a millimeter or perhaps a millimeter and a half in some cases). If you look at the formation of the sutures, you can see which way the bones move in relationship to each other. It took Dr. Upledger a while to make this discovery — or rediscovery.

"At first we just studied the cadavers in the anatomy lab, and it looked like the bones were fused together. But I have a friend who is a neurosurgeon — he would take bone samples across sutures from living people that he was operating on. He'd take a very thin slice, quick freeze it, and overnight it to us in Michigan. And we learned to study these things with different kinds of stains. There was no chemical invasion here at all, no phenol or formaldehyde or anything. We saw the structure of the suture was very capable of movement. Then we measured it on monkeys, and it moved very well on monkeys. Then we found out it was a singular hydraulic system. I would put just a little pressure on the tailbone of the monkey and I could stop the motion of the skull bones. I would do this because of the connection and the hydraulic force that I was able to exert, increasing the hydraulic pressure just a little bit."

So sometimes Dr. Upledger works on one area of the body that will actually be treating a problem on another part of the body. That's probably going on at least 75% of the time in good CranioSacral Therapy. "I am an osteopath, so obviously I've learned spinal manipulation too, and we have a lot in common with chiropractic in that aspect of our education. I don't think there's much argument about that. What I like about the sutural movement is that if the suture does not move, we know there is something wrong. Then we do things to make it start moving. In cranial work, you don't have to work hard, you don't do any thrusting or any sudden pushing. You just resist a movement in the place where it's moving hard, where it has the most motion. Then the hydraulic portion in the inside will open up that stuck suture for you."

In his book Dr. Upledger states that you use no more than the pressure of a nickel. That's five grams, which you hold for a period of time. This is a pumping action. The volume of the fluid is going up and down about ten times a minute inside the skull. Cerebrospinal fluid Volume — there's the pressure. In any hydraulic system, if you push in one place, the force you use is being broadcast throughout all of the fluid.

"You can use the rise and fall of fluid pressure, and I'll get to how that happens", he says. There's a suture that goes across the top of your head like a pair of earphones would come together. That's the coronal suture. Let's say that it's stuck because your forehead has been jammed backwards because you fell down and you banged your forehead. You jammed that suture together. Now the compensation to allow for the rise and fall of fluid volume inside may be taken up in a suture that runs up along the back of your head from side to side. Now he examines it and finds that the two bones, the frontal and the parietal bone, (where you got jammed) are not moving, and the compensation is happening in the suture which is a couple of inches behind that. So if he puts his hand on the back one and holds it together with just a little bit of pressure, and then let that pumping action of fluid on the inside work on the suture that's stuck, it will gradually begin to open that suture.

That's how this works, we are taking the compensation away in one place, reducing it, and that causes the hydraulic force to go to the other place. If you really know how this works and you understand the anatomy, you get so you can direct force all over the place. Now, what causes the pumping action to occur? "What we found out first of all is that the sutures spread and close, as I said, in about ten cycles per minute.". Now in the saggital suture, which is the suture that separates the two halves of your skull (it runs front to back down the midline and it starts about four inches above your eyes), there are nerve receptors that stretch and broadcast the stretch. They also have compression receptors so that when the two bones come together and press enough another signal is sent. The signals go down a nerve trunk we discovered that runs down through that membrane system which separates your brain into right and left parts. It goes into the ventricles of the brain and gives a signal down there. In the ventricle system of the brain is what is called the choroid plexus and that plexus extracts fluid from blood. In other words, it uses osmotic pressure and some active extraction, but blood flows through capillaries on one side of this system and it extracts just the fluid and leaves the cells, so it takes kind of a blood plasma out. Actually, it's a little more selective than that. It doesn't allow all of the ions to pass through. That is the manufacture of cerebrospinal fluid."

The cerebrospinal fluid is made from blood at a certain speed, say "speed 2x." Now there's a constant reabsorption going on of the cerebrospinal fluid back into the bloodstream at the rate of 1x. The reabsorption stuff is located in most of the venous channels in the skull itself. The reabsorption system is called the arachnoid system. The arachnoid reabsorbs the cerebrospinal fluid and puts it back into the blood. Blood comes into the skull, some of the fluid is extracted from it, and it becomes cerebrospinal fluid. At the same time, some of that fluid is being reabsorbed. It's only reabsorbed at "speed 1x," half as fast as it's produced. Obviously the volume increases, and when it does the suture on the top of your head is expanding. It has stretch receptors up there. When it stretches to a certain point it sends a signal down that says stop making fluid and then it stops. Reabsorption continues.

As the reabsorption then brings the fluid volume down again, the suture begins to close. When it hits the compression receptors, the message goes down to turn the production back on. What we found is the production is on for about three seconds and off for about three seconds in a normal situation, which gives you about a six-second cycle.

It's caused by the literal physical pressure in the suture either compressing or stretching. The switches that turn on and off control the production turning on and off, and that's what causes the motion to occur at ten or twelve cycles per minute. It varies a little bit from person to person.

Dr. Upledger says he owes Delbert Smith, a patient, his whole career. He found something calcified, a coin-sized shape on the outside of his membrane, and noticed that it had a rhythmic pulse which was different from the breathing machine or the heart rate machine. "I thought that was very fascinating — it had a rhythm but it wasn't related to the other two! At this particular juncture I could visualize the rhythm of the other two systems and this was different. It stuck in my mind because I could not hold this membrane still for the surgeon to scrape the tumor off. He was pretty upset with me. But he turned out to be the same surgeon that sent us the skull bone samples so that we could prove that sutures could move."

So this is a system in the body that's obviously always been there but no one was really aware of. Cranial osteopaths knew about skull bones moving, but they didn't understand this system. Dr. Upledger saw this thing in his patient, and he knew that there was something different that he didn't know anything about, and nobody else in the operating room knew anything about it either. Then along came a piece of literature from the Cranial Osteopathy Academy.

"When I was in school osteopaths were considered kind of offbeat quack types. Most of the people in our college wanted them to hide because they were considered an embarrassment. Everybody knew skull bones didn't move (as far as the school was concerned), but these guys were getting some clinical results: they didn't know why the skull bones were moving, but they knew they were moving. I had the opportunity to see what was making them move during surgery. Most of the guys that did Cranial Osteopathy never did much surgery. Most of them were a bit more elderly, and osteopaths until the 1940's weren't doing much surgery. So what happened was, I took a position they had offered me at Michigan State to research several things. I researched Kirlian photography, acupuncture and Cranial Osteopathy. We came up with how this whole thing works and actually the Cranial Academy didn't like the idea because it was like heresy against the mainstream of their organization. My job was to put a scientific basis underneath it and either prove it or disprove it. That's what our dean wanted me to do. I proved it was there, but it was different from what they thought it was. So, we did discover this system as it is, and we called it the craniosacral system."

Dr. Upledger was in private practice for almost twelve years in Clearwater Beach, Florida before he was in Michigan. This is where he saw Delbert Smith. Then he went up to Michigan State in 1975. They offered him a job as a clinician/researcher and he accepted it and was up there for over 8 years. Later on he taught at the Menninger Foundation in Topeka, and one of the people from Unity Church heard him there and asked him to start a model holistic health center there for Unity Churches. He took that job for three years. Then he started his own institute, in 1985 in Palm Beach Gardens, Florida.

In CranioSacral Therapy, the treatment is fully done hands-on, and the evaluation, too, is done hands-on. "There's an example I can talk about where the patient doesn't have any problem with sharing. An Olympic diver, Mary Ellen Clark. She won the bronze medal on the high platform in Atlanta. Mary Ellen was suffering from vertigo (dizziness), which is common to high divers. She had been all over the country. She came to see me in September in hopes that she could make a comeback. She had to lay off diving for about four months prior to that. So I evaluated her and I'm looking for stuck places in the craniosacral rhythm or the way it broadcast through the body. Her problem is dizziness, so she's been treated by all kinds of ear, nose and throat specialists and other doctors, but nothing worked. She couldn't dive. So I scanned her body as we would do in a craniosacral examination. What I found out was a lot of the problem was coming from the lower end down at the sacrum and up the dural tube (of that tube of membrane) into the head and then restricting the right temporal bone. This in turn was causing her to get dizzy, because your balance mechanisms are located in the temporal bone. The normal mobility of 10-12 cycles per minute motion was restricted in that temporal bone. Now, it wouldn't do any good to move the temporal bone if you don't get the reason why it's stuck. That came from down in her lower back. Tracing from her lower back what I wound up with is she had an old injury in her left knee that was coming muscle-wise and fascia-wise up into her low back, restricting her sacrum. That was compromising the activity of her craniosacral system, which in turn was screwing up her temporal bone and making her dizzy. I got her knee fixed and then everything else was a piece of cake, and she was back to diving again. And then she won the bronze medal at the Olympics."

When Dr. Upledger was at Michigan State he did a lot of work with physicists, biophysicists particularly. While he was working there, one of the things they did was they had Wednesday morning meetings and they had five clinicians and twenty-two PhD's from a wide variety of scientific backgrounds. They had already gone through the suture movement and had the hydraulic system pretty well taken care of. Working with these patients he said, "You know, I feel like there is an energy transference between the patient and myself when I am working with them." Part of that, he says, is because you have your hands still on them. You use maybe a little pressure on one finger, and then you move this or that, but your hand stays essentially in the same place, so that the hand/skin contact on a patient (or through the hair) is pretty constant. At the same time, he was doing research with Kirlian photography. What he was doing was taking Kirlian pictures of his fingers and his patients' fingers on the same place before and after every session. He did this for a couple of years. What he noticed was, that if you came in with severe back pain and he worked on you, the first Kirlian picture you would probably have very weak coronas or defective coronas, which is the name for the broadcast of the energy out. He might have strong ones, but at the end of the session maybe you got strong or full corona and he got more defective. It would look like he had lost some energy to you. Now the question becomes — and he threw this at the physicists — can we measure that kind of energy transference? For a week or two the physicists ignored this question, and then he told them if they knew what they were doing, they would be able to answer this.

One of them started watching Dr.Upledger with all of the patients. He was there all the time. "What did you do that for, why'd you do this, why'd you do that?" Ultimately, they wound up studying and making recordings of full body electrical potential, tuning out such things as electro-myographic stuff. What they were looking for was the body potential of fluctuations, considering that the body has a bag full of electrolyte conductors and the skin is the insulator that keeps it inside. "When I do certain things, just by positional changes or modifying the cranial rhythm by compressing one area that's moving too much, that kind of thing, it would change the electrical potential of the total body as we were measuring way down in the lower limbs. What he taught me to realize was when I found the right position with a patient to reduce the pain or to take that pain away, the electrical potential that he was measuring would drop when I got in exactly the right place. If I kept it there long enough the electrical potential would start to come up a little bit. He said, "How did you know how to find that place?" It took a lot of introspection, but finally I discovered that when I found exactly the place that took the pain away, the craniosacral rhythm stopped. It stopped at the same time that the body electrical potential would drop. What we discovered here was that there is a change in electrical potential when I find exactly the right position. Now how did I find the position? Well, my answer to that was that I just followed the body's tendency. What we found out over a lot of arduous work was that if I was very skillful and very sensitive, I could find the position. I would go with that body to a position that alleviated the pain. It was the body that was taking me there. Then we found out those were the positions that the injury had occurred in initially. It happened over and over again. These were mostly Worker's Compensation patients, and they were mostly work injuries that I was working with at the time. The patient would say, "Gee, that's exactly the same position I was in when I fell down and hurt my back!" I didn't know that. Carney didn't know that. The patient didn't even know it until he got into the position. So we called that "tissue memory" because the muscles are taking us exactly where we need to go. When we get there, the path of injury is a straight line. In other words, if I fall down on my tailbone on a step, the force of me hitting the step goes into my body in a straight line. But when my body is straight, that line is bent. The energy can't come back out again around a curve or around a 90 degree angle. When I get the body in exactly the right position, that straight line is once again reestablished, and now the energy can come back out the straight line. We found out when we measured it with thermography that we would get one or two degrees centigrade increase in heat while the body was releasing and at the same time during that period of heat release, the millivoltage was down and flat and I had a stop in the craniosacral rhythm. When the heat started diminishing, the cranio-rhythm started again and the electrical potential came back up — not usually as high as it was before, but back up to maybe halfway to where it was before. We got a correlation between all three of those things. So I learned a lot of physics then. Carney started bringing books home from the library and said, "You learn this, and THEN I can talk to you." I really appreciated it. He was a good teacher. Anyway, we decided that what's probably going on here is we have a chaotic energy that comes in — this energy from the blow comes into the body and it's disorganizing. Your body may dissipate it and then you don't have an ongoing injury. If the body can dissipate that foreign energy when it comes in, fine, you'll be all well and the tissues heal in maybe a week or two. It's those injuries that last that are the problem. You fall on your tailbone and you never get better."

The injury happened at such a time or such a way that your body was unable to dissipate that foreign energy — so it concentrates it into the smallest possible ball. When we find the pathway that the ball will exit, then the pain is gone. We call the compression into the ball an "energy cyst." Actually, Elmer Green from Menninger called it that. I was describing it as "entropy" and he said, "You are describing an energy cyst," and that's more correct. The tissues remember how to take you there, and when you get to the right place, it's like the body tissues are saying, "If you'll do this with me, I know how I can get this thing out of here." If you follow the body and do it very sensitively, it will take you to exactly the right position, the energy cyst comes out, and that thing that's been giving you trouble for the last five years is gone."

They used to do a cardiac monitor and a breathing monitor and then a total body electrical potential monitor in both limbs. They had electrodes which Dr. Upledger decided arbitrarily to put about three inches above the kneecaps on each side and then ground each one on the same side at the top of the foot. That way they were as far away from brain electricity and heart electricity as they could get. Carney made a special instrument that would add the negative and positive fluctuations. He tuned out what most electomyographers would term "noise." Carney edited in such a way with his instrument that it turned into a pattern we could read. Then they decided they would study the heat output when they saw this energy was coming out, and the Kirlian photography gave a general idea of whether the coronas improved or not, whether or not the patient gets better.

For non-practitioners or lay people to work on one another, Dr. Upledger has something called Share Care Workshops. Those are conducted not just at the Institute in Florida, but around the country by different practitioners.

Dr. Upledger thinks that bodywork is going to really thrive and the reason for that is because conventional healthcare is going more and more high tech and more impersonal. He had a patient just the other day that had a virus infection that invaded his brain and they had him in the hospital for four days and nobody came closer than six feet to him. Everything was done by MRI's and all that kind of stuff. No doctor came in and really touched this guy. "The human situation is such that we crave communication with someone on a touching level. When someone is a bodyworker, if all they are is well intentioned, and sensitive to the needs of the person they are working on, they can impart a level of self-healing that can't be done with a machine. What I really see happening is a big polarization."

There are some people that are really hooked on machines and high tech stuff, and there are other people migrating towards bodywork because it involves person-to-person contact. Not only because of that, but that's the thing that they really crave. Bodywork will become more educated also. The more you understand the body and the more you work with it, the more you find out that you can facilitate bodily self-healing. A lot of people are getting very tired of paying big bucks for all those pills.

Bodywork is the vision of health care that gets more and more popular, simply because of the interpersonal relationship if nothing else!

■ ■ ■

16

John Robbins

HEALING THROUGH ORGANIC FOODS

John Robbins is the best-selling author of Diet for a New America and May All Be Fed. He is an educator, pioneer and founder of EarthSave, an organization dedicated to the transition to more healthful and environmentally sound food choices.

For many people Organic agriculture is just something that is an outgrowth of the hippie movement. It's something that's fringe or marginal. This is the kind of the attitude you get in some parts of America. But from a global perspective, the organic explosion is extraordinary. The European Union probably leads the global organic explosion with a 35 fold expansion in organic area since 1985 — with an average annual growth rate of 30%. Organic agriculture now accounts for 3% of the total European Union agricultural area. There are other areas that are even higher. In Austria for example, 13% of the farmland is now organic. There are other European nations, such as Sweden, Finland, Switzerland and Italy that are also leaders. In those countries 5-10% of the total agricultural area is now organic. It's really sweeping the world.

What's happened is retail sales of organic produce and products in North America have been growing 20% annually. They are now at about $10 billion a year. It's driven by market forces. It's consumer demand. But in Europe you have two forces driving it. You have consumer demand; people who are not willing to expose their bodies to pesticide residues and not wanting to contribute to poisons in the food chain and the water and soil and farm worker exposure and so forth; but also, in Europe there is substantial preference and support. The growth in organics in the United States has come in spite of virtually no government support.

Organics is growing rapidly in the U.S., but not nearly as rapidly as in Europe. This is very important thing to realize. Europe has witnessed the Mad Cow Disease (in the United Kingdom), and therefore people are much more conscious and much more concerned about food safety and whole foods than they are in America. They don't want to buy foods that are genetically modified and are not labeled, that have been irradiated and are not labeled, that have been filled with poisons and are not labeled. In Europe the genetically modified foods have to be labeled. In Japan the same applies. Actually, in most of the industrialized world that's the case, but in this country the biotech industries have fought that successfully.

Tonnes of pesticides are shipped abroad and come back in our imported goods. This is called the "Circle of Poison." Some of the worse pesticides, particularly the chlorinated hydrocarbon pesticides (the DDT family) are extremely long living in the soil. They don't break down, they don't biodegrade. They accumulate and concentrate in the food chain. They go up the food chain, and are very toxic, very dangerous substances. As such they have been largely banned for use in food production in the United States. But they're still manufactured. There's been no decline in production. Now they are shipped to other countries, particularly Latin America, where they are used and then exported back to the U.S., which is why it is called the Circle of Poison.

Commercially grown bananas, coffee, tropical fruits — produce in general for that matter — grown in Mexico and Latin America are likely to carry extremely high concentrations of the most poisonous of the pesticides. Therefore, people who are trying to reduce their exposure need to be aware of this. You should really think twice about consuming commercially grown produce.

By and large the developing nations are stuck in American wake, and Europe is the most aggressive toward change — but the rest of the world is where America was a generation ago. Although there are some exceptions. In Cuba partially as a result of the boycott, there's been a nationwide shift to organic markets. There's over 30,000 urban gardens which produce vegetables for city dwellers. It can be done even in countries which are not the most industrialized. In Uganda, oddly, there has been a doubling of organic agricultural area in the last 5 years. Actually Uganda, which is a small backward country, now produces 10% of the organic cotton on the world market. Believe it or not, Uganda is producing more organic cotton than the United States!

In the past five years organic production in Argentina has jumped 7000%. Argentina will be exporting more than $100 million in organic products this year. In Africa there is an organization called the Export Production of Organic Products Association started in Mozambique and Tanzania, now also in Uganda and Zimbabwe. Everywhere else in the world, there is a tremendous recognition about the value of organic farming. It is there amongst the U.S. population as well, but the United States Department of Agriculture does not deem developing organic agriculture relevant.

In the San Joaquin Valley, you'd have to replant everything and do away with monoculture (because the bugs love that one giant crop). Monoculture, being a very large area growing only one crop, is not a natural way of growing things. For example, if you have thousands of acres of only cabbage, the cabbage moth can wreak havoc. It does take some shifting of land, but there's no law that says you have to plant thousands of acres of cabbage with nothing else interspersed. Recent studies have shown that yields from organic production are comparable to conventional methods, especially over the long term. When you combine that with the high prices organic produce often fetches, and the money that the farmers are saving from not having to pay for the pesticides, organic systems are becoming generally more profitable. There was one recent study regarding organic grain and soybean production in the midwest which found that organic systems were often more profitable even without the price premiums; because of the low input costs, the greater diversity of products being sold than available under monoculture and a greater yield stability.

"Without monoculture you avoid that problem of maintaining insects and parasites that resist the pesticides. It's a huge problem. We are actually losing a greater percentage of our crop to pests (the very pests our pesticides target) than we did before we ever used pesticides, because bugs have mutated and developed resistance. Their lifespans are very short compared to humans. They go through many generations very rapidly, and that gives them the opportunity to develop resistance and mutate, and they've done it; just as surely as the micro-organisms have developed resistance to antibiotics. Then they develop second and third generation pesticides that are more toxic, and create more problems. All of this, by the way, is poisoning our farming communities and causing a great deal of health problems amongst the farm workers. This is something that is sometimes hidden from consumers because they only see the product in the supermarkets and in the restaurants."

The groundwater and the downwind crops are also affected, and eventually everyone is affected. When pesticide-based agriculture was first developed, they hybridized what they called the Green Revolution. It seemed like a miracle, because we were suddenly doubling the crop yield. It's actually similar to injecting some amphetamine into a human being. They are going to suddenly feel a tremendous rush of energy. If they don't have some sanity and common sense they may think, "Oh this is incredible! I'll just plug into the energy of the universe." But a drug induced addiction is not stable and it's not sustainable, and it's not healthy. In agriculture we have become addicted to chemicals in the form of chemical-based fertilizers and pesticides.

We're eating foods that are laden with chemicals but lack nutritional value. For example, the synthetic fertilizers replace the nitrogen and phosphorous and potassium which are the three primary mineral requirements of the plants, but they don't replace the boron, the molybdinum, the great plethora of micro nutrients and trace minerals. It looks good, it's big, but it's not nutritionally balanced.

Eighty years ago (and still in traditional indigenous cultures today) women had their first menstrual cycle at the age of 17, sometimes 16, sometimes 18. This is traditional. This is how the human being seems to have been designed to develop. But in Western cultures today we have a large number of girls 8, 9 and 10 beginning their menstrual cycles. The average in this country is 11 1/2 right now. This has been directly traced to three things: the increasing fat level in our diets; the use of hormones in animal production (particularly in beef production); and thirdly, to the presence in the environment of certain estrogen mimicking chemicals.

What we do to each other, we do to ourselves. What we do to the natural world comes back to us. It's not just a New Age cliche but a fundamental biological law. We're learning the consequences of ignoring that we are all one.

There are people who try to exploit the organic movement and use it as a marketing scam, but the backlash against those who try to exploit the turf deceitfully has been very severe. People have known that the integrity of the word "Organic" is critical. If that's lost then everyone loses. Interestingly enough, a few years ago the FDA recognized that every state had its own version of organic standards, and that most companies operate along the same line, saw the problem there. The Organics Standards Board was set up to arrive at a definition of Organic that would allow for a true national base and standard. But then the USDA proceeded to totally ignore them and come forward with another idea which would have included sewage sludge, and genetically modified stuff, and irradiated food as "organic." This would have diluted the term, and totally pulled the rug out from under the Organic Industry. The Chemical Manufacturers Association is behind that. However, what happened was extraordinary. The Secretary of Agriculture received over 280,000 communications, an all-time record for a Federal official on a given subject. They were all essentially saying the same thing: "This is not organic; you're screwing us! Don't do it!" He recognized it and this is one of the great examples of citizen power, the citizenry opposing a corporate agenda. Although we don't have it finalized yet, it's very clear that the National Organic Standards will not allow the inclusion of sewage sludge, will not allow the inclusion of genetically engineered material and will not allow for the inclusion of irradiated products.

We were "digging our graves with our teeth" as Dr. Andrew Weil says. "Think about medical costs...think of the extra costs of organic produce as true health insurance. Bananas are a great example. They cost more, and they don't look as pretty usually. But the bananas, being tropical fruits, are grown commercially in Central or South America, where toxics sprays are allowed. They are extremely toxic. Sure, you can peel the banana, but some of the toxics are absorbed through the skin. Furthermore, a lot of these poisons are systemic. They're taken up by the plant into every cell of the plant, which you then incorporate into your body. In the long run the advantages to your physical experience in terms of suffering and in terms of medical problems are probably vastly greater than what it's going to cost you in terms of higher prices at the cash register."

You contribute to the rebirthing of a more conscious way of living.

■ ■ ■

17

J. S. Maiden

HEALING THROUGH MEDICINAL HERBS

"I have travelled every part of the world, done deep studies and collected important information about the medicinal plants of more than 100 countries but the most diversity I have seen in medicinal plants is in the flora of India. You can not even compare the medicinal flora of India with the flora of whole world," wrote Dr. J. S. Maiden in one of his famous books on medicinal plants.

From ancient times the Indian medicinal flora and traditional knowledge about these plants have attracted researchers, herbalists, scientists from around the world. In ancient Indian history it is mentioned that many such researchers have visited India in search of this valuable knowledge.

When did ancient man use medicinal plants for the first time and what was their name? This question is still unanswered. Also there is no scientific document available. In India, Rigveda is most authentic document in this regard. In Rigveda, the description of Soma is given as first medicinal plant used by ancient man. There is still confusion about the scientific name of Soma. In Indian systems of medicine, generally medicines of plant origins are preferred to medicines of animal origins. One possible reason for this was the presence of natural flora in abundance in the surroundings of ancient man.

In Ayurveda, it is clearly mentioned that any patient can be cured with the help of herbs present in his surroundings. There is no need to go far in search of medicines. It is also mentioned that 'Herb talks or expresses'. According to ancient literature, by observing a particular herb minutely, you can understand its utility for different human ailments. By their deep studies, ancient Indian herbalists have found that the shape and size of different parts of herbs resembling different human organs, are useful in treatment of the diseases related to that particular organ. For example the Karela (Momordica charantia) fruits look like the pancreas of the human body. In Ayurveda, it is mentioned that Karela is the best remedy for diabetes meliatus. As is well known, diabetes is a result of disturbed activities of the pancreas. Today the whole world is recognising the medicinal properties of Karela fruits.

Similarly, the seed of Akhrot (walnut) resembles the structure of the human brain. Ancient Indian herbalists have mentioned the use of walnut to increase the activities of the human brain. There are thousands of such examples mentioned in ancient literature.

Here is one more example. It is the flower of Aak (Calotropis gigantea). Aak is a valuable medicinal plant and has a reputed position in almost every system of medicine. Like all herbs , the plant of Aak also expresses its utility for humans. It is said that if you see the structure of Aak flower carefully, you will see the figure of a patient, bowed down, and whose spinal cord is stiffened. Apparently, this figure resembles the patient suffering from rheumatism sitting in front of the herbalist and complaining about his/her problems. Aak is one of the best remedies for this disease. The figure of the patient in Aak flower also resembles a patient suffering from sex-related diseases and due to guilt, sitting with his/her head down in front of the herbalist. Not surprisingly, Aak is also a valuable remedy for sex related diseases. Ancient Indian herbalists have collected, researched and documented these types of uses and Indian literature is replete with this knowledge.

According to the World Health Organisation (WHO) more than 1 billion people rely on herbal medicines to some extent. The WHO has listed 21,000 plants that have reported medicinal uses around the world. India has rich medicinal flora of some 2500 species. Of these 2000 to 3000, at least 150 species are used commercially on a fairly large scale.

■ ■ ■

18

LARRY DOSSEY

THE POWER OF PRAYER

Larry Dossey, M.D. is a well known authority on spiritual healing. He lectures throughout the world and has been a frequent guest on Oprah, Good Morning America, CNN and The Learning Channel. Dr. Dossey is responsible for introducing innovations in spiritual care to acclaimed institutions across the United States.

Dr. Dossy describes three eras of healing in his book, Reinventing Medicine. They basically are his way of making sense of all the confusion and chaos going on in medicine today. Era One began in the 1850s and 1860s. Today we call this mechanical medicine. It's the use of drugs, surgical procedures, radiation and it's obviously still with us; it dominates medicine. But beginning in 1950, or thereabouts, a new era began which he calls Era Two. Today this is known as mind and body medicine. It used to be called psychosomatic disease. Basically, it's the idea that our emotions and thoughts, and feelings can affect health.

Era Three includes the ability of consciousness to reach out beyond ourselves to make a difference in other people. Intercessory prayer is an example of an era three therapy–healing intention. Gaining information from the world, such as through premonitions and dreams, that are relevant to health, is also an example of Era Three. These three categories differ radically in how they view consciousness, and how they acknowledge, or fail to acknowledge, cosmic consciousness. Cosmic consciousness is virtually absent from Era One. It makes an appearance in Era Two, but is limited to your own body. In Era Three, consciousness is freed from the body, and is freed from its limitations in space and time.

For Dossey, consciousness is a huge umbrella under which many things gather. He thinks consciousness is infinite, immortal, and eternal;

the equivalent to what many people call spirit. "I use "consciousness" in such a broad way that it includes the concept of spirit," he discloses. "Meditation is a powerful way of entering into healing states. Herbert Benson, for 20 years at Harvard, has shown that meditative states, and almost any kind of contemplative state, can be good for the body. When people meditate, the blood pressure comes down, the heart rate falls, immune changes take place in the body, and so on. So meditation is certainly a way of bringing about healing influences in our own body. But this certainly doesn't approach non-local, or Era Three type influences– where the influence escapes our own body, and reaches out into the world. This is actually been tested in certain studies, and has achieved positive results. For example, at the University of California San Francisco Medical School, they actually tested healing intentions, which were initiated at a great distance by several individuals, for people with advanced AIDS. This was a double blind study. The people who received the healing intentions statistically did much better than people who did not. So this is not just fantasy. This is a valid phenomenon, which has been tested."

Shamanism, for example, Dossey considers non-local to the core. Shamans, he maintains, are good with local therapies too. For example, shamanism is wound up with the use of native methods, including herbs, and so on. Plus, he believes, shamans are excellent psychologists, some of the world's best. He considers shamanism a beautiful mix of local and non-local therapies.

"The Transcendental Meditation movement, popularized by Maharishi Mahesh Yogi, has done many tests on the ability of people to lower crime rates through group meditation, and improve the quality of life in geographic areas. And with positive results, they claim that if the square root of one percent of the population enters into a particular framework of consciousness, then these changes happen. Actually, these studies are very intriguing. They have been published in first rate journals, scientific journals from time to time. They support the idea that group consciousness can make a change in the world for the better," Dossey stresses, but he believes we shouldn't put these techniques in a box, and look at them as an individual therapy, or a group-related therapy. "The studies show clearly, in my judgment, that the intentions of single individuals can make a difference. And also that the intentions of groups can make a difference. So it's both the individual and the group."

Although we often hear about the different parts of a human being broken into the spirit and the mind, and the body, and the emotions, for

Dossey there's such a fluid interaction between them that it's difficult to put them in a box and separate them one from another. There is a kind of a structural relationship between them. Consciousness is over everything. It informs the body. The ancient idea that the physical derives from the non-physical is a valid way to approach this. In other words, the body is contained in consciousness. Not the other way around, which is what's said in Western science. "So, I see the Absolute, my term for the Divine by the way, over everything," he says . Consciousness is under that, and then the physical derives from that. So there's a kind of hierarchy involved. This is the approach that's taken by virtually all great wisdom traditions.

The very idea that you can use any therapy--whether it's Bach flower remedies, or penicillin--apart from, and separate from, the actions of consciousness that go on at the same time, is an idea that's really in trouble. To try to assign some fundamental influence to a certain remedy, or even listening to Mozart, and separate that from what consciousness may be doing at the same time, is virtually impossible, he says, as if these things did not interact with each other.

Is it then better to use all the modalities together? Playing Mozart is good, Bach flowers may be good, and so is penicillin. Then the very idea that we could use something, such as inoculation, is in trouble. He illustrates this view with an example: "If you go to your doctor, and he writes you a prescription for penicillin, you may regard that as a physical therapy. I mean, that's a chemical. But the moment you take the prescription in your hand, you begin to use your own powers of consciousness, in terms of your expectations of what's going to happen. Suggestion, or positive thinking may enter. And, who knows, your doctor may pray for you, or send you healing intentions. 'I want my patient to get over this.' He or she may do that when you leave the office. All of those enter into your clinical response, when you take that pill. I don't think that therapy is as simple as we often make it out to be. Whether we're trying to assess penicillin, or herbal remedies, or anything else."

However, Dossey is not a believer in "energy medicine." He has written widely about his belief that the term is misconstrued, particularly when it comes to the non-local forms of healing. For example, a Qi Gong Master tries to interact with someone at a distance, and people call that today a form of energy medicine. No one inside of science, or outside of science, has been able to demonstrate any exchange of energy in that situation, Dossey maintains. This is a metaphor, he says, which people talk about as if it's real. We talk about sending energy, and talk about subtle energy. There isn't any evidence that energy, subtle or otherwise, is exchanged. "I think it's misleading to call this energy medicine, because that suggests that something measurable and tangible is being exchanged, when the evidence suggests otherwise. I think that our vocabulary has got us into deep trouble regarding how we think about these kinds of therapies. They are expressions of non-local mind–because all of them involve intention, and willing, and the images and visualizations of healing, and so on. Here's the key point: non-local mind, non-local phenomena, are widely known in physics now. But they do not involve the exchange of energy. Nothing is sent in non-locally correlated events. So, what's happening? Consciousness is everywhere; it's omnipresent. There's no necessity for anything to go anywhere, because consciousness is already everywhere. We don't need to lapse back into these old classical images and metaphors drawn from mechanical physics, which is what this whole movement of energy medicine is wallowing in. I've challenged people to go beyond this kind of thinking–to get out of the energy straight jacket. It really does distort how we think these things happen. And coaching things in terms of these energy concepts short changes us spiritually. It separates us. It says for example, "You're there in Sebastopol, and I'm here in Santa Fe. And if you want to do energy healing on me, you're gonna' have to send something to me, because you and I are separate. We have to bridge the gap." And that's where we insert subtle energy, or some form of energy. This is a devastating image, because it separates us."

Non-locality brings us together. It says that these things can happen in principle, because you and I are not separate–our consciousness is already one. So there's no necessity for you to send any sort of subtle energy to me. As long as we call this stuff energy medicine, we're engaging in the images and ideas of separation. This is terrible in Dossey's judgment–terrible because it doesn't fit with ancient wisdom, which recognizes the great unity between individuals at the level of consciousness. It short changes us because it denies the interdependencies in each of us, which is unitary to the core. It consigns us to a world of separation and distance, instead of one that's in unity. "For all these reasons I wish we could go beyond these images of energy healing and energy medicine, which I think need to be abandoned. That's a general comment. I just disagree with folks about that," Dossey argues.

When the group's chanting "Om," they're not sending energy to another person, Dossey says, but stimulating the energy that they have already, like triggering a resonance response. Energy talk is okay to describe what's going on in your body. We all know that there are electrical and chemical energies that are operating inside human bodies. But to describe what goes on between you and me at great distances, energy talk is helpless to describe that. We've got to go beyond the energy metaphors to describe how the influence happens at a distance.

How distant intentions work, how love works, how passion works, how prayer works at a distance? It's an action of consciousness, Dossey maintains. It's a non-local, distant action of consciousness, which doesn't require energy for its activity. Nothing is sent, nothing goes anywhere.

But all sorts of things happen to the patients. Things are being played out in their body as a result of your healing intention, and your prayer, and your loving thoughts, your empathy, etc. In these studies in distant healing, in intercessory prayer, for example, all sorts of things happen, things that can be measured. Disease often goes away. Heart attacks heal up, many things have been demonstrated as a result of the healing intention. Qi Gong Masters are people who are praying, trying to heal at a distance. They often describe energy-type changes in their own bodies. "For example, healers often describe their hands as being warm. They experience tingles through the body. These things are energetic phenomena happening in the body. The distinction I'm trying to draw for you here is that there are these local changes in the body of the initiator and the recipient. But there are non-local phenomena that bridge the gap, which cannot be described by any sort of energetic electromagnetic signal. Actually, it is not easily articulated in common language."

People are completely unclear about this, says Dossey. And they don't distinguish between what's happening in the body of the sender and the receiver–and what happens in between. They lump it all together. And it comes out as some super unintelligible mish mash. And it's killing us, as far as how to carry these things into modern hospitals and medical institutions, which is what I want to do. First of all, there isn't any measurable evidence for any kind of energy that bridges the gap. So this gives the sceptics and the cynics open season. And they'll say, "Here are these people talking nonsense about subtle energies being sent between people...this field is just as crazy as I thought it was." It really hurts those of us who are trying to legitimize this field, and bring it into eventual mainstream medicine, which is crucial. This may just seem like semantics to somebody who doesn't care what you call it. But if you go out into the real world, and you try to make a difference in the highest levels of medicine, you'd better care what you call it. Because the vocabulary and the concepts you use will either make or break it.

This is why this subject has been very important to Dossey, and why he gets rather irritated at the loose language that people in this movement use who do know about science. He wants to say, "Come on guys, sharpen this thing up here. I mean, this is really getting pretty loose here." And unfortunately the response of some of the folks to what he has had to say is, "Well, you're denying distant healing." Or, "You're denying that this stuff is real." Which is utterly not true, he concludes.

People who don't have a positive mental attitude, or, are less spiritual may have a harder time healing, according to Dossey, but it's certainly not hopeless. For example, if you have a group meditation session …you can have a healing influence on those people regardless of what they think. Whether they have a negative attitude, a positive attitude, or something in between. "How do we know this? You can test it. By now, there have been enough experiments with enough people to show that healing intentions operate regardless of what the individual thinks. I think that positive attitude–what we used to call faith, and what doctors now call the "placebo response"–I think that empowers any sort of healing, whether it's penicillin or prayer. But it's certainly not essential. Most of these studies that I'm referring to have been double-blind, which means that the recipient is not even aware that he or she is being prayed for, or being sent healing intention. The healing intentions work any way. So there you go. Plus, you can do these things on animals. You can even pray for a bacteria to multiply faster in these 100 test tubes, versus those 100 test tubes that are controlled, that don't receive healing intention. And those that are offered the prayer or healing intention grow faster. Presumably bacteria don't think positively or negatively."

Dossey's work has been has involved the spiritual aspects of healing. Gender is not an issue when it comes to healing effects from prayer intentions. If there's any area where gender is just rendered almost irrelevant, it's in the area of distant healing, or spiritual healing. But based on scientific literature, and the studies in this area, most of the healers in the experiments are women. There's an openness on the part of women for spiritual healing, that seems to exceed that of men. Dossey is also fascinated by the fact that 50% or more of many of the medical school classes these days are made up of women. Women are bringing a greater openness, and a willingness, to go in the direction of spirituality in medicine. This augurs very well for the future. Women by and large have an intuitive, nurturing instinct that feels quite wonderful, if you're a patient.

Although women think that cancer is their main cause of death, actually heart disease is the cause. Many of the things that women do to prevent cancer, also prevent heart disease according to Dossey. Exercise is an example. Exercise is a potent retardant to both heart disease and cancer, of all sorts. Another example is the use of antioxidants. Many of the therapies designed for one of these problems has a beneficial effect for the other.

Dossey left his private practice in 1988, and at that time medical intuitives were not very widely known. In his book, Reinventing Medicine, he talks about three medical intuitives, Caroline Myss, Judith Orloff, and Mona Lisa Schultz. Medical intuitives are enjoying a comeback. But this is nothing new in medicine, by the way.

Medical intuition is what Dossey calls non-local knowingness. It's gaining information from the world out there, non-locally. Distant healing and intercessory prayer, for example, praying for somebody else, that's inserting information into the world out there to make a difference. It's like extracting information from the world out there. So they go together.

"Women have a greater openness, and a greater willingness to step forward on these issues. But I don't want to leave the men out of this, you know. I really do not want to make this a gender issue. Men have been great medical intuitives also. In my book, I talk about what in the early 1800's was called "snap diagnosis," which is where a doctor simply gives a diagnosis of the patient, without any information, without ever seeing the patient. This was a "guy thing." This may infuriate people, but it's an historic fact. This took place in the medical schools of Europe in the early 1800's, where you had all these male professors in the medical schools competing with each other, about who could be the best at this game of "snap diagnosis." They were incredibly talented. Some of them could tell the diagnosis by just thinking. Some could tell the diagnosis just by looking at a drawing of the patient. They could even tell you the occupation."

A lot of the feminine intuitive instincts are overwhelmed by the experience of becoming a doctor, says Dossey. "I look forward to the day when women cease to knuckle under to all the masculine pressures that are difficult to contend with in medical school. When that day happens, I think medicine is going to change very quickly. One of the key developments is the increasing number of women in medical schools. In some schools, 50% or more of the class is made up of women. What we need is for women to claim their feminine instincts, and their innate ability for nurturing, for intuition, and for empathy, and defend them, and stand up for them. And cease to allow them to be battered down by the masculine pressures of medical school. This is not easy...women pay a great price, as do men for that matter, on entering medical school. When women begin to stand up for who they are in the educational process of becoming a doctor, the face of medicine is going to change dramatically."

Dossey thinks the sense of sacredness can be reclaimed in medicine. And medicine can remain scientific as this process develops. "If you go back in history, you see that early scientists were deeply spiritual, and believed that science could be a spiritual pursuit. For example, the 17th century scientist, Robert Boyle, who gave us Boyle's Law–he recommended that scientists do their experiments on Sundays, as part of their Sabbath worship. You see the sense of sacredness coming out in studies in distant healing and intercessory prayer. I know one researcher–who's a woman by the way–who says that when she does these prayer experiments in her hospital and clinic, she feels as if she's walking on holy ground. This goes to the idea that when you do an experiment, you're opening the window–for the Absolute, God/Goddess, Allah, whatever you want to call it, to manifest. So I'm convinced we can recover the sense of sacredness, as we are already doing by bringing spirituality back into hospitals and medical schools."

Beginning with his best selling book, Healing Words, Dr. Larry Dossey brought increasingly widespread public attention to scientific studies that support the healing effects of prayer. In his later book, Be Careful What You Pray For . . . You Just Might Get It, Dossey took on the question of prayer's potentially negative effects, exploring the conscious and unconscious ways that people attempt to adversely effect their fellow humans.

A 1994 Gallup poll found that five percent of Americans admit that they have prayed for harm to come to others. Dossey found it not only surprising, but shocking. Like most people, he had presumed that individuals uniformly used prayer for good. But this survey clearly showed that they did not, and it was a very disturbing sort of finding. If you do the arithmetic, you can see that over 10 million Americans are out there praying for harm for others, and that's just the one in twenty who will admit it. If there were 10 million Americans who had some illness, it would be called it an epidemic. So it's an epidemic of negative prayer. In the healing arts, any intervention that can heal can also harm in certain circumstances. This is also true of prayer. There have been studies in which individuals have tried to harm certain cells in the laboratory. An example is trying to kill cervical cancer cells. This has been done. People can actually kill or damage these cancer cells, under controlled laboratory conditions. So the bottom line is that this is not an illusion; this capacity exists and it is quite real. The example of the cancer cells is illuminating, because it shows that, if used wisely, this ability to kill or harm or damage living tissue can come in handy. It can be used to heal. Most of us, if we had cancer would love to be able to kill those cancer cells. It's when we direct this power to innocent living things, that it becomes a side effect, or malevolent. Unfortunately, that's what those one in 20 Americans are doing. They're actually trying to manipulate, control, or harm other individuals. So it's not prayer that is the problem. The problem is the person doing the praying. It's how we choose to use prayer that is the problem. Like penicillin, this stuff can cure or it can kill.

There are times where it can do harm inadvertently, times when the person is not intending to do harm to the person they're praying about, but where it might have harmful effects anyway. "People do this without thinking. For example, if I say to someone who cuts me off in traffic, "Damn you!" or "To hell with you!" this is a negative intention that one could even say is a form of negative prayer. You could reinsert the religious language in that invocation, and say, "I pray to the powers that be that you be damned to hell!" That's a negative prayer, and we ought to be more responsible about that. Some people have written to me after reading this book, saying that they have gotten in touch with the potential negative implications of the offhanded comments that they make to people in the course of a day, and don't even think about." That's something Dossey wants to raise in the minds of individuals who read his book.

The most famous, even legendary, study of positive prayer is the one by Dr. Randolph Byrd which Dossey discussed in Healing Words. It's not a perfect study, but it got everybody's attention. This study looked at the ability of prayer to make a difference in people with heart attacks in a coronary care unit. However, from a purely scientific point of view, the most precise studies are not in humans. When prayer is used to affect non-human beings like bacteria, yeast, plants, or germinating seeds, studies can be controlled with tremendous precision. And these studies show clearly that the prayers and empathic thoughts of people can affect these living systems. This is powerful evidence. There is no way to dismiss these studies, and combining thenon-human studies with the human studies, you come up with a powerful package, which suggests that prayer can have distant effects, even when the recipient is not aware it's being offered.

The NIH Office of Alternative Medicine (OAM) funded a New Mexico study on the effects of intercessory prayer for people undergoing rehabilitation for substance abuse. OAM received a lot of flak for even funding such a study. The study was inconclusive. The dropout rate was so high that only tentative conclusions could be drawn. There was no positive effect found for prayer, and as a matter of fact, there was a suggestion that prayer could have negative effects. For example, those patients who knew at the beginning of the study they were being prayed for by loved ones, actually drank more than patients who were unaware whether they were being prayed for. "Dr. Scott Walker, who did this study, picked the toughest group of patients to do a prayer study on that I can imagine. When people pray for alcoholics, it is probably with a divided mind. They may pray that they stop drinking, but they may also have another agenda, which goes like this: The alcoholic has ruined not only his life but the life of his family, he has done this willfully, and deserves whatever happens to him. People may be offering a superficially positive prayer that he stop drinking, but they may also have a hidden agenda that is quite negative — that he's a bum who deserves whatever happens to him. So Dr. Walker has suggested that we speak about "tainted prayer," because such prayers may be tainted. So which prayer wins out? The prayer that they get what they deserve, or the prayer that they stop drinking? We come here to the issue of the unconscious mind in prayer. Walker's study is important, not because it resolves any of these issues but because it raises them."

We are such complex beings that we are often out of touch with our unconscious, which can wish negative things for people, in contrast to what our conscious mind may be saying, Dossey asserts. "In view of this, I think we ought to reevaluate how we pray. For example, instead of praying for something specific, we might ask that the highest good prevail in the situation. We might pray, "May Thy will be done," instead of trying to dictate the terms to the universe, or using prayer to micro-manage our lives and the lives of other people. We are so horribly informed about some aspects of our own physiology, that it bedevils how we pray. Two good examples are people with allergies and autoimmune diseases, who are out there praying for an increase in their immune strength. Well, these are diseases of too much immunity. Why on earth would we want to pray for more immunity if we've already got too much? So one can bypass all these technicalities and complexities by ceasing to spell it out in prayer, and by asking a greater wisdom than our own to take care of the problem. By praying for something general instead of something specific, which, as I said, is best exemplified in the prayer, "May Thy will be done," or "May the best thing happen in this situation." There are situations where praying for somebody without their permission is justified. For example, if a person is unconscious, in an emergency situation where consent cannot be obtained, or if the subject is an infant and cannot give informed consent. One can imagine that it's okay to pray for others in these situations without their consent. However, as I've discovered to my dismay, there are quite a number of people out there who do not wish to be prayed for. I underestimated this problem; I thought everybody would love to be prayed for if we could show that prayer works. This is not the case. They say they resent the condescending, patronizing, controlling attitude of people who are praying for them. They say that people who are praying for them are trying to manipulate and control them. They say their psychological space is being invaded. There have actually been lawsuits threatened against people for this. So it raises the issue of informed consent and prayer. As a general rule, I think it's probably wise to ask permission for prayer if we intend to use prayer to bring about specific changes in that person's life. However, there's a way to leap-frog all these complexities about informed consent. If we were to pray, simply, "May the best thing happen for this individual, may Thy will be done in his or her life," we're not putting our trip on that person. We're just asking in a loving way that the best thing happen for them. If we pray this way, I fail to see why we need to obtain informed consent."

There is a fascinating study on long-term survivors of AIDS, in which people who were able to say no when asked by a friend to do a favour that they didn't want to do had more active immune cells. That work comes from Dr. George Solomon of UCLA, one of the giants in the field of psychoneuroimmunology. Indeed, people who were able to say no did better with their AIDS. They had greater numbers of immune cells, and did better clinically. This implies that standing up for yourself, not letting someone push you around, stopping being accommodating, are important attitudes in doing well, probably not just with AIDS but with any infection. "I think it's a better way to go through life than letting people stomp all over us. There is this attitude among a lot of spiritual people that goes like this: I'm so enlightened and spiritual that it's okay if you just walk all over me. Solomon's work suggests that this is a horrible attitude to take. There is a point for warriorship, for standing up for what you believe in and not being pushed around. Living your life for you, not for someone else."

Anger is also a very complex issue, according to Dossey. There's righteous anger and justifiable anger. Anger can, however, shade off into hatred, which is not good. Anger that is legitimately based, and has a psychologically justifiable reason to exist, is certainly a very valid emotion. We belittle anger, and focus too much on empathy, love, and compassion. But there is such a thing as tough love and assertive compassion. So we need to honor that hard edge to human emotions. I think we ought to value it.

Dossey recounts this healing story: "The astronaut Edgar Mitchell's mother was legally blind. She could not drive without glasses. She attended a conference her son was involved with, in which there was present a healer from the Orient, who Edgar asked to work on his mother. His mother was a born-again Christian, deeply devout. Overnight, after the healer worked on her, she woke up and her vision was normal. She could see without her glasses and could read fine print. And she stomped her glasses into smithereens, just to demonstrate that she didn't need them. Well, she drove back the hundreds of miles after the conference without her glasses, so there was no question that she could see. Then Edgar got a call from her. She was disturbed by the Oriental sounding name of this man, and it had begun to occur to her that he must not be a Christian. Edgar confirmed for her that he was not. The mother began to think that since the healer wasn't saved, he must be an agent of the devil, and she disavowed any healing effect he had had on her. Very quickly, her vision deteriorated, so that she once again could not see without glasses. This is an amazing story, It suggests that out of religious bigotry and narrowness, people reject healing. Oddly enough, they can even do it in the name of Jesus, who was the Great Physician. I think this story is extremely instructive. What we call religion can actually interfere with healing."

Dossey thinks we have to respond to bigotry and narrowness and religious intolerance with compassion and love. Most of those folks are not mean people. They're trying to do the best that they can. We have to embody in our own lives the principles that we preach. We must respond to them not with intolerance and anger, but simply with patience and compassion. He think that if we do this, and we continue to sing our song, that sooner or later we'll see a movement toward some middle ground. At least that's the guiding light in his own life.

"As you might imagine, people have come out of the woodwork from organized religion to condemn some of the things that I've stood up for, such as the fact that no religion has a monopoly on the power of prayer. This horrifies a lot of fundamentalists, who believe that they have cornered the market. So I have encountered in my own life the question of how to respond to people who believe that you are an agent of the devil. I pray for them. I continue to focus on what I think is good research, and I try to share this information in an even-handed, loving way with people."

Dossey suggests that we have a psychospiritual immune system, which works to protect us automatically from the negative thoughts and intention of others, pretty much the way our immune system protects us from infection. It operates invisibly and behind the scenes. But sometimes it needs to be supplemented, and we do look around for things to do to add to the innate protection we have.

Dossey thinks positive prayer is one of the best antidotes to negative prayer and the negative thoughts of others. He discusses positive prayers that could perhaps do the job. One is the Lord's Prayer. There's a clause that says "deliver us from evil," which many people regard as a potent prayer of protection. The 23rd Psalm, and the Prayer of St. Francis are others. Imagery and visualization can play a role in protection. Imagery and visualization are part of prayer for almost everyone. It's virtually impossible to pray without using some kind of imagery. Being surrounded by white light, or a protective, monolithic wall through which nothing can penetrate, are images which have been used by people to good effect. But Dossey warns against getting too exotic with forms of protection. "I know people who have gotten sucked into really far out forms of protection, where they become so paranoid that they devote all their time to trying to get protection. I'm not an advocate of chanting exotic, magical words from Persian astrology to protect yourself. Those things may work for people in other cultures, but I think the rule for people in our culture is to keep it simple."

The most important developments in alternative medicine in the past 5-10 years, according to Dossey are the following: "One is that the disappointing failure of orthodox medicine to handle the chronic illnesses of our day has propelled this field forward like no other. Also, the increasing recognition that the role of consciousness, the role of decision-making and personal responsibility, is paramount. And the realization that you can actually use science to demonstrate the effectiveness of various forms of alternative therapy. We really can develop proof that these things work. But, it may well be that the most powerful incentive toward these directions is utterly mysterious. I do not basically understand why our culture has opened up so dramatically to these new directions. It's almost as if there's some dynamic that is "doing us." I don't think that these directions are all rational. I'm not unhappy about that. We'll take these movements any way we can get them, whether they're rational or not. I doubt that we can specify all of the reasons why this is happening now. I'm just happy to be along for the ride."

■ ■ ■

19

LAMA SURYA DAS

HEALING THROUGH BUDDHIST SPIRITUAL MEDICINE

Lama Surya Das is the most highly trained American lama in the Tibetan Buddhist tradition. He is the author of several best-selling books including Awakening the Buddha Within and Awakening the Buddhist Heart. His work communicates the wisdom of Buddhism for the modern-day spiritual seeker.

Lama Surya Das is a lama in a Tibetan Buddhist Order. But although he is a lineage holder in Tibetan Buddhism, he teaches Buddhism for the West including non-sectarian but mainly Tibetan Buddhism. Being a lineage holder means that he is a trained and authorized representative and transmitter of the tradition, not just "I like Tibetan Buddhism, and I saw the Dalai Lama on television once."

Buddhism is an old religion, older than Christianity, so over the centuries and millennia it developed different traditions in different countries and cultures. It's like Catholicism and Protestantism and then the new religions in America such as Mormonism, Baptist, Christian Science, that came out of Christianity. Buddhism has different schools, sects, lineages; some monastic, some lay, some traditional.

Some are more reformed or experimental and it's different in each country. As Buddhism moved from India to Nepal and Tibet, then to China, Japan (where it became Zen), it evolved and changed.

It follows the same tenets and practices and the three enlightenment trainings and ethics trainings. Plus the meditation trainings and wisdom trainings. Tibetan Buddhism has Tibetan Yoga practices, Dzogchen, massage and things that don't exist in any other part of Buddhism. Zen

Buddhism emphasizes chanting and visualization, and energy work and healing work more than other forms of Buddhism. Tibetan Buddhism emphasizes philosophy, and Buddhist logic and mind training.

The Dalai Lama is the head lama, the chief, not exactly the pope because Tibetan Buddhism is not that hierarchically structured. In general, he's the head of Tibetan Buddhism.

Surya Das was a student of Dalai Lama and organized conferences with him with the International Buddhist Teachers Conference.

In Tibetan Buddhism there is a being called the Medicine Buddha, who is an ancient healer. Unlike the historical Buddha, the Medicine Buddha is more like the historical Buddha taking a visionary form. It's called Sangye Menla in Tibet. He's depicted as being lapis lazuli (blue-like) in colour, holding healing herbs in his hand. The Tibetans consider it Dharma, which heals what ails us on all levels, spiritually as well as physically, emotionally…so that this Tibetan Buddhist medicine actually coming from what we call the Four Medical Tantras taught by the Medicine Buddha, and which forms the foundation of Tibetan Medicine. It's related to the six yogas of Tibet and other practices that includes purification, fasting, special diets, astrology, collected herbal formulas and medicines.

This teaching included four levels of medicine and the highest or fourth level was Spiritual Medicine. Spiritual Medicine is regarded as providing the deepest healing because it's related to the idea that healing at the soul level heals you for eternity.

Working on the spiritual level brings us more into our eternal home, and gets us in touch with our natural state of inner health and completeness; beyond birth and death. In other words, you may be very sick, but soul healing will bring you into peace even though you might die of the illness. You can be healed that way — not healed and live forever, because nobody can live forever, but healed spiritually, which transcends birth and death and goes on. We need to realize that we are deathless.

In this lifetime, we're helping our spiritual growth by focusing on the spiritual, but the spiritual focus also helps with mental, emotional and physical ailments.

As discovered by Dr. Larry Dossey people who have a better attitude are more loving and respond better to physical treatment. That's the point of spiritual healing; it's a generally a more holistic approach than the allopathic, cover-it-up kind of healing. Recognizing, for example, that stress and tension, anger and negative emotions and so on contribute to illnesses of various kinds. Love and friendliness and unselfishness also heal on other levels and connect with our inexhaustible souls. Violence and aggression harm ourselves as well as others, so it hurts us in various ways. We need to heal the divisions between ourselves and others. That's why the Buddha said something like "Love and kindness is the greatest medicine." One of the meanings of the ancient word Dharma is "that which heals." (Usually we talk about Buddha Dharma, meaning Buddha's teachings or Buddha's wisdom, but that's one of the etymological meanings.)

As far as the Medicine Buddha goes, there's initiations and empowerments you can receive from lamas to extend your longevity and vitality and help you heal — and particularly, to help you practice the Medicine Buddha meditation yourself. So you can actualize and develop your inner healing capacities on yourself and on healing others.

In his books Surya Das suggests developing spiritual intelligence which is innate in all of us. It's a matter of how much we develop it; just like we all have muscles, but some are flabby and some are firm from exercise. Spiritual exercise helps us develop our spiritual muscles. We can develop our spiritual intelligence in various ways: by thinking and connecting more to the bigger picture, rather than just living for instant gratification or seeing things as separate and discrete events, without recognizing the bigger patterns and universal laws. We should see these connected to ourselves and others. It is about bringing spirituality into our relationships through all of life's connections. We should develop our spiritual intelligence by finding our spiritual center either in ourselves or a religious way, thanking Jesus or Buddha or God or service or yoga or meditation or prayers as the center of our life.

"This should be our focus point and there are lot of ways to do this. We need to distinguish the real from the unreal and go more towards the Light and away from Darkness. Then we can start to understand the universal laws of cause and effect and why things happen. Once we understand our karma, we can be masters rather than victims of circumstances and conditions. We can be more grateful for all that's given and not just take it for granted. We need to recognize our precious human existence as a cherished life, and prioritize the now, and respect and cherish life in all forms. And practice non-violence and so on. In a way, we could do a spiritual IQ test and see what our spiritual IQ is; where we are as far as selfish or unselfish, loving or hateful and mean-minded, generous or tight fisted and so on. This is regardless of what "ism" you believe in, or even if you're an atheist or agnostic but have some humanist sensibilities."

In his books Surya Das claims that we're blessed with life. But there are a lot of people who don't see life as a blessing. What does he say to them? "As Buddhists we don't proselytize. We only teach when asked, so people need to be questioning, so we can discuss things. If people are asking, then we can explore and inquire together to see if human life is a blessing or a curse. And maybe we can count our blessings and not just feel resentful, bitter or victimized. So if people are stuck and they're not enjoying life, they should ask for help from the spiritual teachers in their community. We have to look at our own belief systems. Are we just seeing the glass as half empty rather than half full? Buddhism is neither optimistic or pessimistic. We try to be realistic and take things as they are. There's a great freedom in that, and with freedom comes responsibility."

Samskaras mean karmic imprints or deeds or habits that are in our psyche; the stored consciousness that Jung talks about. In other words, the imprints that are in us and push our boundaries, so that we react in a conditioned fashion the same way to certain stimuli. It's like the stimulus/ response reaction, which keeps us from being free. When somebody says critical or nasty words about us, we instantly react and get mad rather than having more detachment or equanimity. We need to be able to consider the criticism in terms of how that might be true and helpful or whether it's false; and thus keep our balance, be centered and mindful rather than just reactive. The samskaras are like the buttons that get pushed as we continually are bombarded by stimuli (outer and inner), and not just from others, but also from our own inner emotions and thoughts and memories. As we become more aware through meditation, self-inquiry and mindfulness practice, we start to have more space and more clarity to be able to manage our reactions and to choose more skillfully whether we kick back or not when somebody steps on our toe. That's the child level of reaction, but we do the same thing at the adult level; if people look at us funny or cut us off in traffic, we get road rage.

So the samskaras can continue with you from one life to the next, negative karma as well as good karma. If we have an intention to serve others, to be a shepherd like the Dalai Lama and the incarnate lamas in Tibet, the physical body can only go so far, 50 or 90 years perhaps, but one can be reborn and carry on that mission. So that's the idea of the reincarnated one. In the case of lamas of Tibet like the Dalai Lama, those karmic seeds ripen in the next life in a positive way, to complete the unfinished mission for the benefit of all.

The Bodhisattva path is the highest spiritual ideal that I've ever encountered. It's predicated on the recognition that we're all one. And the common ground of all beings is that we all want to be happy and well, and have our loved ones be protected and safe and happy and not harmed. We're all joined in that way, therefore we dedicate ourselves to the greater welfare of all, not just for our own selfish, temporary welfare in this short life. When we take the Bodhisattva vow, we make ourselves a spiritual servant, like a saintly or peaceful warrior working for peace, enlightenment and the betterment of all beings. And not just human beings, but all beings of all kinds throughout all lifetimes, in all possible worlds and universes. It's really a saintly, cosmic aspiration of service and dedication to the highest good for all (as opposed to the temporary gratification or the materialism of this life). That's really the basics of Tibetan Buddhism; the Mahayana Buddhism, the Great Vehicle or Great Boat. The vehicle intent on universal liberation, not just individual relief or individual enlightenment. It's realizing that as long as any being is suffering or is imprisoned, I too am not completely free. So we pray, "May we all together complete the spiritual path. We vow not to go to Nirvana or complete our spiritual work until all beings get there." So as long as there is any suffering in the world, there is still spiritual work to do. That's the Bodhisattva vow and the Bodhisattva aspiration and that's the heart of the Mahayana Buddhism.

All lamas take the Bodhisattva vow. It's common in Tibet, China, Japan and other Mahayanist countries. But there are Buddhists everywhere who take it, not just in Mahayana countries. It's not just an ordination amongst the lamas.

"I urge my students to take this vow everyday. We take refuge in Buddha, Dharma and Sangha; the teaching and the practice of Enlightenment. Also, when we take the Bodhisattva vow we're not just thinking of ourselves selfishly; we totally include all beings in our prayers and practices and in our heart's embrace, so that we dedicate ourselves selflessly in service and altruism and compassion as well as wisdom. The vow says "Sentient beings are numberless, I vow to liberate them. Delusions are inexhaustible, I vow to transcend them. Dharma teachings are boundless, I vow to master them. The Buddha's way is unsurpassable, I vow to embody it." That's the Bodhisattva vow, the four lines from the Japanese Zen Tradition. The best part is you can say it everywhere, even if you're commuting in traffic or you're on a long trip, or you're waiting for a meeting or an elevator, a movie; you can just say it to yourself. It's a good way of integrating spirituality into everyday life, not just waiting until you have time to sit down on your meditation mat and do it in the morning."

We have to learn not just mentally but physically, such as with yoga. And we have to learn emotionally through attitude transformation or therapy or other kinds of spiritual work to see through our self-illusions and our limited self-concepts and find out who we truly are through self-inquiry and introspection. This can help us out a lot. Dream work and dream yoga while we're sleeping (knowing we're dreaming) can help us a lot. This opens subconscious storehouses so we can come to a more full appreciation and understanding and then finally acceptance of ourselves and of others. We're all working to transform and become better people in a better world. Of course, we want to be better people, live a better life and contribute to a better world…but acceptance goes a long way towards helping us to be more clear and more centered while we go about that good work. Otherwise we support the contradictions and hypocrisy like "fighting for peace" which is a contradiction in terms. We need to make peace with ourselves before we can work for peace in the world. We need to think globally about these big issues, but begin working locally, with ourselves and each other. There are actually Buddhist practices like loving kindness and compassion meditations that include forgiveness and love and kindness to yourself. They really help us forgive and remember, not forgive and forget; and learn from our experiences. We can become wiser with years of experience and accept and forgive and be more patient and gentle with ourselves. There's a lot of learning we can do in that way, through loving kindness and compassion meditation.

There are self-esteem issues that many of us have that are left over from youth, and that can undermine our courage to do bigger tasks of service. So until you're happier with yourself, you can't take as deep a breath and jump as high, whether you're just working to be a millionaire for yourself or to serve the world. If you're unhappy with yourself then you can put on a smiley face and do good work and all that, but it's kind of like having termites gnawing at the foundation of the house. So there's a huge cost that ties up a lot of our energy, which brings us back to the health question. These issues gnawing at us inside; they are keeping us tense and preventing us from being authentically ourselves, being open and vulnerable and truthful. There are all kinds of games we play based on fear. We're hiding.

There are all kinds of persona we project; all kinds of co-dependence and narcissistic syndromes, not to mention heavier things like addiction and pathological behavior.

When you say you're going to serve all beings consciously with the Bodhisattva vow, that includes yourself. Otherwise you're just sort of draining yourself. You can become a martyr, like the co-dependent wounded healer.

"Jesus said, "It is not what goes into a man's mouth that defiles him, but what comes out." I think there's a lot of damage we do with our mouths and with our words; with lies and deception, but also with gossip, sniping and slander. We are unconsciously doing all kinds of damage, so practicing Right Speech is one of the steps on the traditional Eightfold Path taught by the Buddha. Right speech, right action, right livelihood, that translates as wise speech, wise action, wise livelihood; it is a part of the ethical and moral training of Buddhism. It's a good thing to concentrate for one day on one step in the Path. Take one day where you really observe your speech; not just your verbal speech but your inner dialogue, your expressions and everything that comes out of you; including your gestures, your looks and glances; and see what you're creating and projecting in the world and its results. This can be very enlightening and enlivening."

The Eight Steps are: right view or right understanding, which is seeing things as they are; second is wise intention, being more unselfish with the bigger mind, bigger heart. So much depends on our motivation and intention even before our actions. Third: wise speech; fourth is wise action; fifth is wise livelihood or wise vocation; growing ourselves spiritually and in every way while we grow our business or our profits. The sixth step is wise effort, not just sweating and straining but also knowing how to sustain and balance effort, and knowing how to relax. The seventh is wise concentration or wise attention; and the eighth step is wise mindfulness, wise meditation; being more mindful, conscious, reflective rather than going through life mindlessly, unreflectively, not learning the lessons of life.

The Buddha didn't really found a religion. The Buddha pointed the way to Enlightenment, and of course it became a religion. It's more of a practice, like an ethical and psychological philosophy of awakening. If you ask how the Buddha got enlightened or awakened, the Buddha and all Buddhist teachers say by the three trainings: Ethics training, Meditation training and Wisdom training.

Anybody can benefit by these healthy, wholesome, intelligent and wise practices, with or without converting from any other religion. "I have rabbis and priests and Catholic nuns who come to my retreats. They want to learn these practices so they can go deeper into their own spiritual life. That's why meditation, self-inquiry, chanting and yoga can be complementary, not contradictory, to their own spiritual quest. So these are very good non-sectarian practices for today. It helps with awakening and illuminating our minds, and also helps to open our heart. It is very important for us today in terms of bringing more wisdom, compassion and love and peace into this world."

It helps us love even those we don't like, and helps us transform stumbling blocks into stepping stones like the cliche we hear "turning lemons into lemonade." In other words, even though we can't change the winds of karma we can learn how to sail with them better. So you don't just float away. The spiritual alchemy is like the tantric transformation that Tibetan Buddhism talks about; where we transform the base metal of our animal nature into the gold of spirit which is its true nature. That's why it's not just a transformation but a transmutation. It is transmuting our monkey-like animal nature into the divine nature: realizing that God, Buddha, the Light is in each of us. Each of us can imitate the life of the Buddha and become as loving as they are, as wise as they are. That's the promise of Buddhism, that anybody who becomes enlightened is the Buddha. And millions have done this. That's the Great Transmutation. We can actually find our inner center so we live in our own inner spiritual thoughts. Spirituality goes wherever we go so we're at peace and one with whoever we're with, wherever we are in a noisy, polluted city or in the beautiful, quiet country or anywhere at any speed. Because great peace is beyond the dualism of noise and quiet. Great peace is something we should experience on a more mystical, inner level that remains with us anywhere.

That's an ancient spiritual principle called Darshan; vision of the guru or vision of God; being awakened by a touch or a sight or a connection.

But the real darshan is the vision of reality or the vision of God. The guru or the temple is just the gateway, so having the picture on the book is like the gateway that resonates with something in you that can access something transcendent. It is a personal thing.

So it relates to developing a loving look in your eyes. You know sometimes people glance at you and you might have a harsh look without even doing any bad speech. It's sort of like beyond right speech. You can bite your tongue but it's pretty hard to hold back your eyes if you're not in a good space. That's probably why the main Buddhist archetype of Tibet besides the Buddha is the Buddhist form of Compassion, in Tibetan, Chenrezig. In China she's known as Kuan Yin. In Japan, Kanon. These are all the same, personifying Compassion.

"The Dalai Lama and my own guru, the Karmapa Lama, are considered incarnations or embodiments of the Buddha of Compassion. Out of compassion Chenrezig's loving eyes are gazing with love over all like the mother keeps the children in sight and guards them that way. It's the Buddhist idea of compassion, not personal desire; rather transcendent divine love, unconditional love, that's the word. This is something in Buddhism that we can develop ourselves by practising Chenrezig's meditation. Through cultivating loving kindness, forgiveness, joy, rejoicing in the success and pleasures and benefits of others. The Four heartitudes or divine attitudes of heart that Buddhists cultivate: compassion, loving kindness, joy and forgiveness; these four heartitudes activate compassion. Compassion is a verb, as somebody said; it's not just an ideal. It means doing something, being unselfish."

We can heal ourselves through love and find completeness in love. And that may not involve another person. It may be between my True Self and I or between me and God, to put it in theistic terms. Of course, we can experience this by being transported by the beauty of nature or a sunset. The arts are a great way of awakening the heart today. Service and generosity, giving of ourselves is one of the best ways, one of the high roads to Enlightenment. It always has been. Kabir, the poet saint of India sang "Try to live the Path of Love."

■ ■ ■

20

LINDA PAGE

HEALING THROUGH NATUROPATHY

Dr. Linda Page is a trained Naturopathic Doctor and Herbalist and the author of many books, including the newly revised and expanded best-seller Healthy Healing. She has appeared on hundreds of radio and television programmes and in national magazines and symposiums. She is currently featured on The World of Healthy Healing on PBS television.

Detoxification is one of the oldest and certainly most effective healing methods known to man. There are many records of it as far back as 5,000 years ago, perhaps even up to 20,000 years ago. People have known for a long time that detoxification, or cleansing the body of a build up of toxins, was certainly beneficial to their health. It's a known health benefit all over the world, and it means clearing out congestion. Especially in the highly toxic, industrial world of today, it means clearing out the toxins in our systems, and neutralizing the acid/alkaline balance of our bodies. This is far more important than we may think because an acid system sets up an environment for many diseases.

Detoxification is far more than purging. That used to be what people thought. For so long there wasn't very much information about it available. People started using it for weight loss. Page was one of those people, because she had fought her weight all her life. You can literally detox yourself to death, and she did that. She was in a coma for quite a while. She died right on the operating table and went through an out-of-body death experience. When she left the hospital she only weighed 69 pounds. Unfortunately, she enthusiastically embraced the wrong way to do this and it is one of the things that led her to write her book so that other people wouldn't make that same mistake. Using detoxification as a purging technique either for rapid weight loss, for rapid cleansing of the bowels or some other reason is not the way to go. It isn't really true detoxification. Like everything else in nature, detoxification needs to be done in moderation and with a holistic approach.

It's important to remember the three things: a)balance, in this case your acid/alkaline system; b) getting rid of toxins that are stored in your body; and c) boosting circulation by getting rid of congestion, particularly in the lymph system.

Some of the best detox programs are not these long, very strenuous, clinical type detoxes — unless you are very seriously ill. A mild, gentle, "spring cleaning" type of detox program is all most people need. It can be done over a long weekend a couple of times a year. The hardest part about it is beginning, because it takes quite a bit of change to your lifestyle. Sometimes a series of short detoxes, one or two over a three or four month period works better than a long detox where you would need to be under clinical supervision.

"When someone asks me who needs to detox," says Dr. Page, "I really can say with all honesty that I think everybody does. For instance, I feel that I live a very healthy life. I am working with the absolute newest supplements out there because I am on the testing range with so many of them. Yet I do it because detox is a technique for staying healthy in a destructive world and that is what we live in today. There are over 30,000 destructive synthetic chemicals in our society today and 25,000 new ones are coming in every year, many of them on the winds from countries that have no safeguards in place, or in our water supply."

U.S. industries ALONE now annually release 24 BILLION pounds of toxic substances that are linked to developmental and neurological problems in US children. We have no way of shielding ourselves other than taking care of our own bodies.

Diet always has to play a part. It is something that we do every day. Of course we take in emotional stresses and we may not exercise, and it all certainly is important, but diet is one of the most critical things. Diet is the first place to start and then you build from there — because diet can also help you out with the stress problems which are certainly growing every year as well.

Herbs and supplements in addition to eating a low fat, primarily vegetarian diet, is what Dr. Page suggests for a mildly detoxifying diet or maintenance diet, a protective type diet. She feels that we can always be protecting ourselves fairly easily with our diet. But when we want to go on an actual period that we call detoxification, she targets it more. For instance, after the holidays, she would target detoxification from fats and sugars. If you feel fairly congested and you want to go on a detox period during the spring, she would target the liver -- and we can easily do this with foods and herbs. Any time you are working with a liver detox you want to have help, vitamin D from sunshine helps. A liver detox works best when you do it through the high sun months. Other things can also be worked on, and she sees that people get the most rapid results when they do some sort of target. A protective diet, however, could easily include something early in the morning like green tea. She drinks green tea every morning for two reasons: because it keeps your liver uncongested, and it also helps in the way that bitter herbs help. she usually add bitter herbs to her green tea in extract form. It is a very easy thing to do and it keeps your digestion flowing; it keeps your whole system flowing, your bowel system regular. That is just one little thing you can do every morning. Of course, green tea has been proven to have weight loss benefits, proven immune power benefits and other things.

Dr. Andrew Weil recommends green tea for lowering cholesterol and also as an antioxidant. Dr. Page believes there is good news and bad news about caffeine. You do get increased metabolism and certainly a little mental boost there. Ginger is not only a bitters for your digestion, there are some new things about ginger being researched. For people that may be at risk for heart problems or heart attacks (both men and women), ginger inhibits the same enzyme, for instance, that puts people at risk for a stroke. It's the very reason that doctors often recommend an aspirin a day for people. Aspirin inhibits that enzyme. Ginger does this with much less stomach problems, digestive and eye problems that come along with aspirin. Also, cayenne and ginger work together in a synergistic fashion. Cayenne boosts your central circulatory system, and ginger gets everything right down to your fingertips and boosts your circulatory system all the way to your extremities.

When you have the whole herb, the plant already has built in a lot of the protective benefits so that you can take the whole thing and get the benefits of the alkaloid or whatever else it is. There is a lot that you lose. Now we know for instance with St. John's Wort, that many side effects are coming out of the standardized extracts.

Some of these herbs like green tea or ginger are part of preventive health maintenance. But they may be cleansing and detoxifying you as well. Dr. Page uses both. Another one is sea greens, sea weeds, dulse, kelp or sea vegetables. They are the detoxifiers of the ocean and they can do the same thing for us. They are also wonderful for weight loss and detoxifying, fat, sugar and lymph cleansers. Spirulina is a water plant as well.

Dr. Page works as a traditional naturopath and is getting better results. This is more important to her than the supposed proven or unproven properties of the plant.

When Dr. Page was in a coma, coming out of the coma, and for all those weeks in the hospital, she felt that if she was getting all those things, she didn't have to eat any hospital food at all. The health food store in town was allowed in green drinks and sea greens and the herbs as well. She felt like she was getting a little transfusion. She says it was just like a deep breath because her body was so down.

"I was only eating five things for several years. It sounded good, but it was terrible. I thought I was losing weight. I look at pictures of me then and of course I was anorexic. Incredibly malnourished...I came out of the fashion world so I thought I should be on a cleansing diet my whole life. I nearly detoxed myself into the grave!"

Because you go from cleansing to using your bodies 'vital reserves after a while. She had no B12 and that is what really gives you cell regeneration. You have to take it in, your body doesn't make that.

The Chinese herb that everybody knows about but may not think of in terms of detoxification is ginseng. It's used widely over there, for reproductive enhancement, anti-aging, detoxification and many other things. Ginseng truly is incredibly popular with everybody. Ginseng is a good detoxifying herb because it clears out congestion and restores that body balance. It is not a purgative but it is a restorer of homeostasis.

Dr. Page has been to several ginseng farms and the farms are all very old. They have now developed a way of alternating their fields so that they can grow more. The Chinese do an enormous amount of importing. Up until just five years ago, 90% of the ginseng grown in America went there.

She has also been involved in creating Ayurvedic formulas in the past. Ayurvedic practitioners are the ones that made the vegetable juice diet so popular for cleansing. American and European traditions were using water fasts at the same time; but water fasts do not give you enough nourishment to maintain in this modern world. Water fasts allow your body to detoxify too fast, dumping out all those toxins stored in your fatty tissues way too quickly. You can re-poison yourself. Ayurveda uses the vegetable juice diet as a popular way to work on body cleansing, and they also popularized yoga and deep breathing. Deep breathing can really enhance a cleanse. "As far as the native American Tradition, most of us know about sweat lodges. That certainly was for body as well as for spirit purification. Her favorite herb from the Native American tradition of cleansing is sage. Many people use it today for a cleanse of the house (burning sage) and of course it was used in the sweat lodges in the same way. Sage will also really boost your immune system. As far as the European tradition goes, she used to work in a spa in Europe. A great deal was devoted to detoxification techniques, mostly water techniques. They would lower you into sweating baths or mud baths. She worked in Germany at a spa where you walked right into the mud pits outside. It certainly was a cleansing technique!"

There's no question that every tradition has a way to cleanse the body. In the Rain Forest, the parasite cleanse is of course a big one because that is what they get, and they are getting even more now that they have become inundated with a western diet. It is like an open environment for all the parasites. They keep the body from being able to fight it.

"The way I feel about it in regard to detoxification is that you should start out using an extract, or tincture in water or under the tongue, and then move into a capsule or a tea. In general you will get a better result if you give your body a lot to work with at first. Most people's cleanses are short ones. I recommend using a one ounce bottle of extract or tincture during one cleanse. Go in descending order. This is best because you ask your body to pick up more at first. That way you get a much more permanent result. Whereas with drugs you normally have to take more and more to get the same results."

How is the descending order determined? Teas are the weakest form. They are very good during detoxification because they can flush your body and flood your body with rinses. Capsules are four times stronger than teas. Tinctures or extracts are either four or eight times stronger than capsules. "I don't think you should take every herb all the time. For instance, echinacea, which is a wonderful lymph cleanser and boosts the

Lymph Cleanse, should not be taken all the time. You should alternate one month on and one month off. Even ginseng works better if you alternate. The reason is not so much that your body builds up a tolerance to it (as it would to a drug), but the whole idea behind herbs is that they enhance your body function. You need to give your body time to use what you have been giving it."

Green teas can be used the year round. One of the benefits is that you can add different extracts at different times. She likes to add the bitters because it keeps her system feeling so free and flowing. She use it pretty much all year round, but uses her traveling time as her break.

■ ■ ■

21

Louise Hay

HOLISTIC HEALING

Louise Hay is the best-selling author of such books as You Can Heal Your Life, Empowering Women, and 101 Ways to Happiness. She is an internationally renowned lecturer, founder of Hay House Publishing and a best-selling author of over a dozen books. She is an inspiration to many in the Holistic Health movement.

Hay had always wanted to help people improve the quality of their lives. Gradually, as she started to print her own books and then do other authors' books, it slowly became a publishing company. It's grown quite a bit since the early days — they have worldwide distribution now. But still everything they publish is part of helping people improve the quality of their lives. Hay House been in existence since 1980. It was incorporated in 1985.

The new edition of You Can Heal Your Life, is striking; every page is in colour. It's bringing in a whole new audience, which is wonderful. People who never picked it up before, picked it up because now it's beautiful. And they do get an opportunity to improve the quality of their lives. Her first book was Heal Your Body, a little tiny twelve page pamphlet in 1976. You Can Heal Your Life came out in 1984. And it made a big splash. It's like life said, "We want this to go out".

From the moment she put her foot on the spiritual pathway it's like she has had no control over her life. She just does what presents itself. And life has decided what it wants her to do. "I'm 73 now and I'm not out there dashing around the world like I did at one point. I have the publishing firm and I do more behind the scenes work now than I do out front. I see tremendous growth coming in holistic health."

They have assisted living now and retirement communities and all of them are geared towards poor health. I get a lot of brochures from these places because they think I'm going to want to come and live with them. And all of this stuff is set up for when you get really sick, we will be there to help you to the grave. And I think it would be wonderful if somebody would start some holistic retirement communities where people could really live out the rest of their days in vibrant health. I think it would be very popular, but someone has to do the first one. It could be a national chain. Yoga, T'ai Chi and meditation should be included for senior citizens. And food! If you go to any of those places the food is so appalling, it hastens you to the assisted part of living. "If you don't eat right and you don't know how to take care of your body, you're not going to have the energy to do anything wonderful. And there's nothing wrong with playing golf, but my God, are you going to spend the rest of your life playing golf? That must get incredibly boring! Why not kickboxing? Just because you're a senior doesn't mean that you can't do all sorts of things. Like aerobic activities. Not that you'd have to, but make it available, and then people are encouraged to try it. On my 73rd birthday I took up kickboxing. I said to myself, why not, let's try it. I'm not sure yet that I'm going to stick with it."

Besides holistic doctors and nurses at a holistic retirement community, Hay would like to see chiropractic, acupuncture, homeopathy…all the healing modalities. And a holistic medical doctor on staff, instead of a medical staff and an occasional holistic practitioner. We should swing it the other way around, she says. "I really love my organic garden. I'm semi-retired; I go in once a week. I have a full-time secretary, and I call the lady who runs the company every morning, so I'm really in touch with things. Yes. I'm interested in the creative part, not shipping or things like that."

It's important to be a good steward of our own little personal home environment — and our land, if we have any, says Hay. We need to do our recycling. "I'm an avid organic gardener. Not a lettuce leaf or leaf from a tree leaves my property. Everything goes back into the earth. I grow my own food, so I know I'm eating well. Everybody wants to know why my plants are so abundantly lush. It's because I feed the soil. If we feed the soil of our own soul than we live an abundant and lush life, too."

Earlier in life things didn't flow for Hay so well…family life, core issues. And at some point she decided to grab herself by the shoulders and say "This is what I want for myself and I'm going to achieve it."

When the student is ready the teacher appears. That's what happened. From the moment she set her foot on the spiritual pathway life has never been the same. That is a key in terms of holistic education — to really Follow Your Heart. The spirit flows out of that. Who wants to do something you don't love for a career? That would be a lousy way to spend your life, though most people still do. Most people work at jobs they don't like. "I've certainly done that in my past," Hay confesses.

■ ■ ■

22

LYNN ANDREWS

SHAMAN HEALING

Lynn Andrews is an internationally acclaimed author who has written 18 books, including Medicine Woman (now in its 39th printing), Jaguar Woman and Crystal Woman. Considered a preeminent teacher in the field of personal development, Lynn is a 21st Century shaman whose words reflect her path, a path of heart. Her work explores the ancient teachings taught by the Sisterhood of the Shields, which embrace the study of global shamanic cosmologies and sacred art technologies. For 12 years, people from all over the world have gathered with Lynn for her annual Joshua Tree four-day retreat. In 1994, The Lynn Andrews Centre for Sacred Arts and Training was created—a unique mystery school designed to integrate the sacred into every aspect of life.

The difference between a vacation and a retreat is that on a vacation, you are going truly to just let everything go. Maybe have fun, play golf, play tennis, etc. On a retreat, you have a form and structure for that period of time. The form is a very important thing. For instance, when she gives her retreats, Andrews has a very definite point of view in mind. It usually comes up in the title of the retreat. For the Joshua Tree Retreat, which she does at the end of every May, she always has a theme. This year it's is called, "Digging for Gold, Transformation of the Spirit." This is about learning how to go into the source of your own being, of your own spiritual personality structure, all of the conditioning that you have had, and to be able to look at that and find the magnificent nuggets of gold that are within that structure, in seminar form.

There are some holistic style vacations available now, like spas, health resorts, new age cruises, that might be in the middle; somewhat structured and holistic health conscious, but different from going on a retreat. Vacations are fabulous, but that's more for rest and relaxation. That's when you've come up against a wall and you really need someplace to go where all you want to do is relax. You don't necessarily want to use your mind to do anything.

A retreat is more work, than just rest. It is certainly in a different setting than what you are used to. One time she looked at the astronauts that were being thrown into outer space in a tin can. After three or four days they had a sense of enlightenment, of God. She thought, how can that possibly be, they are up there and they are very busy. It's most likely because they have been ripped out of their daily routine in life long enough so that something new had the opportunity to come in. We are so busy in our lives. We never get a chance for peace, for play, for an opening, where something very valuable, perhaps, is on the edge of your consciousness, knocking, trying to get in there. On her retreats she takes you into a completely different experiential environment so that something new really does have a chance to come in.

Andrews has an event that she does in Hawaii that is much more of a rest. She give things and has people go through experiences together but the style is different. And the space between the different things that they do is very different. They take long periods of time to go and do projects out on the land that work with the spirits of nature and the devas, the little people in the trees, and the water babies in the ocean, and so forth. But it is much more contemplative.

During retreats people are looking for information, a way to see life differently. "When we give our events, we script them. We have magnificent music by absolutely extraordinary musicians, like Scarlet who was with Bob Dylan for years. We use people that have incredible abilities to inspire with sound. We do a lot of work with sound, looking for another way of seeing reality. There is so much in life all around us that is not visible in our normal vision. Shamans talk a lot about "Seeing"; being able to see the energy fields around people, and to see the power of the earth and begin to really work with the energies of the constellations and the stars. When we are at Joshua Tree out in the desert, we have magnificent things happen there. We have had eagles circle around the lecture area. We have had double rainbows. We have had people healed of so many emotional and traumatic events in life. I think when you gather a group of people together who are of "like spirit," kindred souls, you can break through blocks that you can't do necessarily on your own. But it has to be something that is structured carefully. I think that with spiritual work, people don't realize that you have a tremendous responsibility to take care how you do things; you have to use a lot of energy and power. For example, a lot of people are ignorant about what kind of energy you use on a person who has an infection or open wound. You would never shoot energy into that wound; it would simply infect it more. What you are trying to do in that situation is implode energy, pull it out, so that it has a chance to heal itself."

In Oriental healing, they take pulses and they either add or take energy away from points. But you don't do the same thing every time. It may be a wound where it needs energy because the person is almost dead. It is always a very specialized situation. I think this is one of the things people need to realize. Everything is a very unique situation, and you really have to know what you are trying to accomplish before you begin.

There is an opening of energy in the universe. The energy has speeded up and we need to let go of what no longer serves us and move ourselves consciously and with awareness into our life's work, whatever that might be. That might just be living with your full consciousness, raising your family, or it may involve activating that power that you have been afraid to do. Now is the time. If you want to write a book, now is the time to do it.

"Whenever I needed to learn in my years of apprenticeship (and as far as I am concerned I am still an apprentice to the Great Spirit) working with the women, if there was an aspect of my spirit that was flawed in some way or my personality; for example, fear of death, something I needed to work with; I needed to make that my ally and understand the beauty of elderhood. I would work with one of the elder women in the Sisterhood of the Shields, and they would take me through a sequence of events and teach me about myself. One of those events was going to Australia and working with this extraordinary aboriginal woman named Ginevee, who taught me a great deal about "quickening." We were out in the desert one night, in the outback alone, and we were sitting by a fire. We suddenly felt the ground start to shake. It was a herd of wild camels that were running through the camp. They came towards us and ran right by us. She said that is what the universe is giving us right now. Time is speeding up and we need to quicken ourselves as teachers, as Shamans, as women being on this earth. We need to quicken up so that we can catch up with those camels running by. The camels symbolically meant the time that is the quickening and that we have to move, and get rid of what we can't carry. If you are going to run to catch up with a herd of wild camels on the run, you have to let go of almost everything, right? You couldn't carry hardly anything. You would have to run. That risk is a great part of spirituality; it awakens the spirit. Many people are very lazy, not only physically but spiritually. They may look very disciplined on the physical level, but they remain spiritually lazy. What wakes that up, that part of you that needs to get going and needs to pay attention, is risk."

Lynn Andrews has two important concepts: "Being committed to your own enlightenment" and also "Removing our masks and seeing our original face." These things seem to be important in whatever age you happen to live in, especially in critical junctures of time. When you talk about the original face, that is what our retreat is all about. It is all about going back and finding that original face, that beautiful being you started out to be, before all the environmental cloaks were wrapped around you. That's a gift. We always think about that as a problem, such as our conditioning as children. Andrews doesn't look at it that way. She thinks it was a gift that you asked for. If you were an abused child, and she was, it was a gift, in the sense that it gave her a path on which she could work. And she worked on that, and walked down that path and learned so many things. Anything that happens to you is a mirror that you actually create. It doesn't just happen to you. She believes you have to take responsibility for anything in your life. If you look at it that way, then all the problems that you have and difficulties that you have become gifts that you work with and solve.

"When we do a retreat, let's say with this instrument of the shield, with my teachers, there are 44 of us, and all of the women are very elder women from all over the world from native cultures. They do not work with traditional native culture at all. They are memorizing a very ancient, powerful and positive lineage of consciousness that has been handed down through the centuries. That is what I have been taught. When I work with them I tell them I am going to be doing this big event, and we sit and we dream and we pray. I see what it is that I feel is needed for people at this time through this juncture of third dimensional consciousness. What I divine is what people need on the retreat. People need something very different this year from what they did last year, I feel. They need to learn to dig for gold within themselves; meaning, how to find that vein of truth, awareness and power that we all have. For this particular year it is transforming "base metal," our emotions, our character into something that is far more powerful, spiritual, and aware.

Andrews' Sisterhood of the Shields is a group of all women from native cultures from around the world. They are native people, very elder. I hesitate to say how elder, but they have transformed through the processes of aging. Andrews wrote a book called Medicine Woman many years ago. In her twenties she was married, had a daughter, was living in Beverly Hills and was looking for her spiritual teacher. She met many, many wonderful masters who were incredibly skilled, powerful and full of heart and soul, but she wanted to learn from a woman. At that time, spirituality was not as easily spoken about as it is today. So she went in search of a teacher and the whole story of Medicine Woman unfolded, where it became part of her destiny to go to the north of Canada and work with Agnes Whistling Elk and Ruby Plenty Chiefs, who became her mentors and teachers forevermore.

She works with them to this day. They are part of a secret society called the Sisterhood of the Shield including women from all over the world. All of these women came together memorizing and knowing this sacred knowledge that came from the stars. They always would say to Andrews, "We are made from the stars and to the stars we must one day return." She thinks this ancient knowledge is Pleiadian, but it doesn't matter; but she doesn't get into things like that because she doesn't feel very comfortable with belief structures (you have to believe this or you have to believe that.) What is important is that you believe in yourself and your relationship to the Divine, whatever that is for you.

Andrews doesn't go into belief structures. When she is giving an event or a retreat, she wants people to come and discover who they are. What is their special little flame inside that makes them the exquisite creator that we all are. We are all part of the Great Spirit. We are all reflections of the Great Spirit. She wants people to open up to their inner selves more than having a belief structure. It is not just their innerselves, it is their own absolute magic. If you believe in magic, it happens in your life. "I am a shaman. I am not a medicine woman. In other words, I have learned about energy. I have learned about how to heal the body with the power of thought, the power of spirit. I think as we are in spirit, we are in the physical body. So, I work a lot with healing the total self. However, a medicine person is affiliated with an ancient tradition, that they are usually born into and raised into; an ancient lineage. My situation is vastly different. I am not Indian. I was not raised in a lineage, and I am certainly not a medicine woman, which implies a very traditional ritualistic background. She is a student of native women but they have not been teaching me traditional native culture. They have taught me a very different, highly evolved cosmological study. We work with the earth. I happen to think that we chose to come here to learn certain things. Thc physical dimension of the relative world, the time-space continuum, is a very powerful teacher, because within this world we can create mirrors. In the process of becoming a writer, for example, you create a mirror that is an undeniable teacher for who you are. I saw in the process of writing my first book, Medicine Woman, that I had not organized myself the way I thought I had. It was one of the most painful things I ever did, because I had not prepared myself anywhere near what I thought I had. It took me a long time to get through that book and to write it because I also was afraid of being successful, afraid of being known. I was an abused child, and if you are an abused kid, you are afraid of putting your head above the ground because you think it will be knocked off. I wanted to be loved. And I thought as a woman, I didn't dare be successful because nobody would love me."

She could see energy forms around people: she knew when they were lying; she could see the red in them when they were angry; she could see where they needed to be healed; but she didn't know what to do with it. She knew it was a tremendous responsibility, but it also separated her from everybody and it was very difficult. She had to find out from somebody what was happening to her, and that is why she went in search of a teacher. She knew she had a destiny, but she didn't know what it was.

The purpose of medicine is power of meaning; that you have power over your own dreams, that you can manifest in the world your true nature, and that takes personal power.

Preparation for a retreat is an individual matter. Some people are very lazy and they need to prepare to get themselves together. Other people are so incredibly busy that they need to do a meditation to clear themselves. "I think clearing yourself is a good idea. In other words, visualize a slate, a blackboard in your mind, with all of this stuff written on it. You see all of these formulas and words and people and things to be done, and then slowly wipe it away. See the slate all clean. Then as you sit there and meditate with it, it will suddenly get filled up again. Then you erase it again. That's peace. On retreat I think it is best to come in knowing what you want to achieve, or you may just want to be open to what happens and let it happen to you. The problem with all of us is that we go into something and we doubt it, we judge it. We think, "I don't like that person; I'd rather be roomed with somebody else; that person isn't paying enough attention to me," and so forth. We need to get rid of those personality things that come up."

The only way the mind can control you is with thoughts, and it doesn't want to lose you to a higher endeavor so it will try and reel you back where the mind has control over you through the thinking of thoughts that structure you. The little simple things you think about all day long are always filled with judgments and opinions. Not that this is necessarily bad, but what you need to do is just let thoughts go through your mind and don't hang on to them. Just let them go through.

After writing 12 or 13 books, Andrews realized that people need so very much. There's such a hunger for awareness, people needing to deepen themselves. At first she thought that the books were all people really needed from her. But as she lectured and worked, she realized that people needed much more. A lot of people that she works with are massage therapists or doctors or healers, and they need to understand certain things. So she thought, maybe she needs to start a school. So she went to the Sisterhood. She sat and counseled for a long time. She told them what she thought was needed and they agreed with me. They helped her along with some wonderful people who worked for her. And they helped her design this process of teaching. She decided to make it a school without walls, a correspondence school, so that people from all over the world that couldn't get to her or to a campus, could still work with this information. They have trainings a couple of times a year and have mentors to work with people, to help in different areas of study. It has become one of the finest things she has seen done. She is so proud of it because she pictured it from beginning to end. She wrote four years of training.

She has a Bachelors and a Masters degree which are affiliated with the University of Naturopathic Medicine at Santa Fe, New Mexico. They also issue a minister's license, which is very important; She doesn't give that just as a piece of paper. She stands behind that training because people often want to create a congregation of some kind. The minister's license enables you to do that. she wanted to have a continuing education program so people could be under an umbrella where everything is created, so that they could do mailing lists, exchange ideas, talk about different lodges that were involved and so forth. They meet once a year and have an absolutely magnificent time. The school has really flowered from what she has planted from seeds into this sacred soil.

She has a website: www.lynnandrews.com. They have forums, shopping clubs, they are even putting classes online.

"Spiritual materialism is very dangerous simply because we are very serious about what we do. We feel that this is the only way, we are on a path and this is it. There is no other way. That sort of attitude is putting a sense around your consciousness, and that will absolutely keep out other endeavors but it will also keep out the truth. When we become spiritually material, we become dedicated to what we do. When you choose a path you need to stay on it for at least 7 years to really learn what is there for you, but it becomes material in the sense that people who are spiritual need to survive in the world. True spiritual materialism is when you lose your perspective of God. Everything is made of light. You are God in a sense, you are the Great Spirit in the sense that you are a reflection of the light of the Great Spirit."

You can become conscious and aware, and as you become conscious and aware, you will enlighten those around you. It is about education, and education sometimes cannot be dealt with in a direct way. Why do people cut down the rainforest in Brazil? How in the holy world do we stop people from doing that? It is through their ignorance that they do such a thing. If they realized truly what they were doing, if they were educated enough about what they are doing, that wouldn't happen.

"I think we need to share our love, share our light, share what we know, without doubt or judgment. Share openly, knowing that you may know nothing. You know nothing and you can heal no one. But, you can love and give of your spirit, and you can enable people to find their own enlightenment."

■ ■ ■

23

NEALE DONALD WALSCH

HEALING THROUGH THE NEW SPIRITUALITY

Neale Donald Walsch lives with his wife, Nancy, at a retreat site they have founded in the woodlands of southern Oregon. Together they have formed ReCreation, an organization whose goal is to give people back to themselves. Walsch is continually touring the country, answering requests for lectures, and hosting workshops to support and spread the messages contained in the book trilogy entitled Conversations with God.

The new spirituality will be a spirituality that's not based on a particular dogma. And that steps away from the old spiritual paradigm that we have created on this planet, which comes from a thought that there is such a thing as being better. The sad part about our past is that religions, ironically enough, are responsible for creating the most destructive idea that has ever been visited upon the human race: the idea that there is such a thing as "better." I question that the word better has any real value as it's used by many religions–and then subsequently by other institutions in our society.

The basis of most organized religions is that they have–their founder or founders have–received a direct revelation from God. The most recent of which is Joseph Smith of the Book of Mormon, as recently as 1867. But many religions traditionally claim that their founders' experience of the word of God is the one true experience. And everyone else's experience of the word of God is at best a mistake, and at worst a blasphemy. And from this construct has arisen a concept that "We are better than them." The Roman Catholics teach that unless you're a Roman Catholic you do not go to heaven. There's an old joke about the man who went to heaven and found three doors and Peter said he could go to any one of three doors to spend eternity: room A, room B or room C. In room A were all the world's Jews. In room B were all the world's Protestants and Peter wouldn't show him room C. And the man said "Why can't I take a look at room C before I make my final choice?" And Peter said "Because in Room C are all the world's Catholics. And they think they're the only ones up here." Beyond the Catholic exclusionary paradigm is a larger one which is the Christian one. Christians claim that if you don't believe in Christ, you can't get to heaven. Well that eliminates two thirds of the world's population!

"One either has to believe in a God who's terribly prejudiced, or disbelieve the teachings of such exclusionary theologies. Religions have taught us that "we are better than they." And because we are, somehow, better than they, we get to go to heaven and they don't. Christians will tell you outright that they believe that. They may not use the word better. But they certainly believe that they'll go to heaven and Jews will not. And this thought of betterness has crept into every area of society, where in fact, it becomes insidious. It begins with our children when they are very young. And indeed as you just mentioned they find themselves on teams."

It becomes "our neighborhood is better than your neighborhood." It becomes "our family is better than your family." It graduates to "our state is better than your state," and "our nation is better than your nation." And it circles all the way around to where it started: "Our God is better than your God." And because we believe that our ethnic group, our society, our political party, our God, is better than your God, we kill each other. The new spirituality will bring about what I'm calling the "end of better."

"And that is in fact what is called for in the next of the series of books that I've been writing. I'm calling my book series the "with God series." And this next "with God" book is Friendship with God. This book challenges us to bring about the end of "better" on this planet. I was told to challenge every minister, every priest, every spiritual teacher, every world leader, every politician, everyone that has a constituency of any kind, to stand before their constituencies and utter the one sentence that no religion, no political party, and no nation on the face of the earth will dare utter: "Ours is not a better way, ours is merely another way." That single sentence would change the experience of the world. That is the new spirituality. That will be the guiding principle. The new spirituality will step away from dogma, will step away from "We're right and you're wrong." And it will step into an inclusionary kind of understanding, that allows us to honor and to celebrate each other's points of view without finding them mutually exclusive."

It is a "unity in diversity" spirituality. We don't want to be homogenous as a race. We each like our own tribal culture, but it doesn't have to be competitive teams. It can just be our individual offerings. That'll be the first characteristic of the new spirituality.

The second characteristic of the new spirituality is that it will produce an experience in human encounters in which we become a living demonstration of the basic spiritual teaching "We are all one." And everything that violates or mitigates against that teaching will not be part of the new spirituality. The new spirituality will also base itself on a third very large spiritual understanding, which is that life is eternal. Most religious people claim to believe that, but very few people actually live as if that were true. In fact we make most of our decisions and most of our choices as if we're not all one, and life is not eternal. As told in Friendship with God, if we simply decided to believe and act as if first, we're all one, and second, life is eternal, it would render virtually everything we've done all our lives pointless. Because our choices are largely based on survival. But if life is eternal, life is not a question. And if we're all one, we need to stop our competition with each other. Most of the decisions we make are about survival and winning. If we win, someone else loses. But if someone else loses, we lose. Which is a point we're not getting. The new spirituality will make this just painfully obvious. It'll become obvious that we've really been working against ourselves. As the new spirituality begins to become the pervasive spirituality of the planet, we'll find that we have abandoned our philosophy of contradictions in which we say we're all one but continue to try to win. And in which we say that life is eternal but continue to struggle to survive.

Things happen individually first, and then collectively. It's not the other way around. Individually we're moving very rapidly toward these understandings. You find individuals agreeing on this, but when they get into collective societies and larger groups they find it difficult to achieve group agreement.

In Barbara Marx Hubbard's book Conscious Evolution, she mentions the phrase "cultural creatives." The number she quoted was 44 million, which means there's a very large group of people waking up.

But not that many are actively working with changing the system yet. "That's why Marianne Williamson and I have formed an organization called the Global Renaissance Alliance. Barbara Marx Hubbard is on the Board of Directors, along with Deepak Chopra and Wayne Dyer and James Redfield, and a host of others. All of these folks have joyfully joined with us to provide an arena within which our "cultural creatives" can identify themselves. And unify their energies, focusing them in particular directions to produce particular results."

As we move into the 21st century, there's what the Bible calls a "quickening of the spirit." In metaphysical terms, it could be called the increasing the speed of the vibration of life. And we're seeing a higher level of consciousness and many more opportunities for people to challenge their present ways of thinking and move into a grander and larger experience of who they really are. That's probably a result of just a general increase in speed of the vibration of life itself.

We've seen in the last half century an incredible shift. This is just an extraordinary time to be alive. A great many people experience the movement from one century to the next, but a minuscule number of people experience the movement from one millennium to the next. It's a very small and select slice of all the people who have ever been born. We've come back during this time, those of us who are here now, specifically to experience it. And to cause a "quickening of the spirit."

■ ■ ■

24

PATRICIA GARFIELD

HEALING THROUGH CREATIVE DREAMING

Dr. Patricia Garfield is an expert on dreaming. She's the author of the best seller, Creative Dreaming, as well as several other books in this field, including Pathway to Ecstasy, Your Child's Dreams, and Women's Bodies, Women's Dreams. Her first major book, Creative Dreaming, created a major social impact because of the fact that she went back and looked at the Senoi tribe of Malaysia, and the unique ways in which they treated their dreams, and suggested that people in the West might learn something from that. Westerners were used to thinking of dreams as something that happened to you, and then you worked with them. You worked with a therapist, or you discussed the symbols, but you waited till the dream was finished. What was different about Creative Dreaming was saying that you can get ready to dream, you can prepare to dream, you can do something within the dream to change your dream. People had just never thought about it that way before. And when they began to try some of these techniques, they found indeed it made a difference — not only in their dreams, but in what happened in their waking lives afterwards.

Garfield had been writing her dreams down since she was fourteen and has a collection of thirty or forty thousand dreams by now, there are twenty-some volumes of these dreams recorded. When she was young, she began to notice that just by paying a lot of attention to what was going on in her dreams, things were happening. For example, in one dream, one of the characters, a young girlfriend of hers, said, "Do you know I represent sex to you in your dreams?" This is in the dream. And Garfield said, "No." She said, "Haven't you noticed I always wear shorts?" At that stage of her life, she thought that was pretty daring. But her dreams began to comment on themselves, and she didn't realize it, but that was the beginning of what we call lucid dreaming — a dream in which you know that you're dreaming, and you can change the action of the dream while it's happening. Many people notice this happening to themselves. For example, one woman told Garfield that when she was little she often had recurrent dreams about a witch, and one night she said to herself, "There's that darn dream about the witch again. I'm not going to wake up screaming. I'm going to stay asleep and see what happens." And just by noticing that you've had this dream before, or saying to yourself, "This is just a dream. I can wake up if I want to," while you're in the dream. This very special state of lucid dreaming can give you a power in your dream state. It's sort of like a cybernetic feedback system. You become aware of the fact that you're dreaming, conscious of the fact that you're unconscious. It seems like a paradox. At first people didn't believe that this was possible, and now we've had a lot of laboratory studies that have proved that in fact some people can learn to do this, can even be trained to become lucid in their dreams.

But creative dreaming is more than lucid dreaming. But one leads to the other. In Creative Dreaming she wrote that there are many ways to use the resource within us. Every night when we go to sleep, four or five times a night, our bodies experience this particular physiological state that has psychological symbolic meaning, but we can learn from this. We can actively use our dreams. That's what she calls creative dreaming — that is, setting up a relationship.

It's remarkable to think that we spend, most of us, a third of our lives asleep, and a large portion of our sleeping lives dreaming, about four years. Four years of a human lifetime dreaming. And it's usually ignored by people. There's an old saying of the Jewish people in the Talmud, that a dream uninterpreted is like a letter unopened.

Yet most people don't begin to work with their dreams at all, or pay them any credence whatsoever. You obviously recommend that people do just the opposite — that there's a lot of value to be had. Many people, though, can't remember their dreams, or they claim they can't.

Remembering your dreams is a kind of memory skill, and anybody can learn it, unless the person is on heavy drugs or alcohol. Certain drugs — sleeping pills, for example — will actually inhibit the physiological dream state, and when you go off the pills, then you have this terrible condition we call a "REM rebound," with very frightening nightmares.

But unless you have this situation, where the person is inhibiting their dreams, anybody can learn to remember their dreams. There are specific suggestions, of course, in Creative Dreaming, to remember dreams. Anybody who's interested in remembering their dreams, just knowing that they can — putting a pad and a pen near your bed so you can write them down, is a good place to start. Just deciding that you're going to remember your dreams can help. And one important thing that's helpful is to keep your eyes closed when you wake up. As soon as you begin to move around, and open your eyes and get all sorts of other stimuli coming into your system, this very delicate dream recall gets broken easily, if you're not used to it. One of the things Garfield recommends is lying still and keeping your eyes shut and just catching hold of the last little bit of the dream, and very often it hooks onto the scene before, and the scene before.

These are very delicate states of consciousness. One of the best arguments for a person to begin to remember their dreams or write their dreams down, comes from Garfield's second book, Pathway to Ecstasy, or The Way of the Dream Mandala, in which she points out that by working with your own dreams, and combining that with various meditative practices, you really are able to enter into an ecstatic state of consciousness, a very blissful state. Not everyone wants to pursue that aspect of dreaming. But those who do find it very worthwhile — that by using the images of their dreams, the special power images, so to speak — they can begin to understand a whole pattern that's happening within them. "I was suggesting their making a mandala out of the very powerful images in your dreams. For example, I used to have dreams about the house that I grew up in as a child. It was a place I hated, actually. I was very unhappy during my teenage years in this particular house. And in my dreams I would often find myself back there in a very negative situation — all kinds of terrible things happening. That was so unpleasant to me, with very thick stone walls, and it was always cold, and had all sorts of unpleasant aspects. And usually the dreams were negative. But after a while, I began to find changes happening in there. Still very powerful dreams, but I might be in the attic going through all kinds of old papers, and suddenly find a very beautiful blue vase, or a lovely picture. The dreams began to change. And this is very important with anybody's recurrent dreams — to look for the little differences."Part of Garfield's method, then, is to look at the horrendous, negative images in dreams, and to try and somehow transform them. That's where the power lies, in effect. Because within the very image that appears to be terrifying, if you get in touch with it, if you begin to understand it, the power that went into forming the frightful image can become yours. You're released somehow from the fear, and translate it into something more creative. You become able to own it. It belongs to you, instead of belonging to the frightening imagery. For instance, if you confront something in your dream that is terrifying you — maybe it's a giant cricket, that's one dream Garfield had; or another where she was being chased by a poached egg; or it can be your standard zombie or Frankenstein or wild animal. Whatever it is that's after you in a dream — it's very common, being chased or attacked in a dream — if you stop and you confront that in any way — anything from saying, "Hey, cut that out. Stop. This is my dream. I can do what I want," or even making friends with it, and saying, "Hey, why are you bothering me like this?" Once she said that to a dog that was trying to nip her in a dream: "Cut it out. Why are you doing that?" And actually, they talk back to you, of course, during the dream. And this one said, "I just want you to pay attention to me." But there was something that she needed to understand in that image, and instead of running away from it, hiding from it, if you face it, if you interact with it, you begin to get some of the strength that's within that image.

"I was teaching this technique to some children, and one little girl said that she was having nightmares about a shark, and he was taking a bite out of her, and she was very frightened. Usually he would kill her. And after we discussed this, she wrote to me and said, "You know, when you first told me that, I didn't think it was possible, but I tried it, and it still was scary. This one bit me, and then I saw myself dead." And I talked to her some more, and I said, "Yeah, but look, you changed the dream. You already made it different. If you can do that much, you can go further." And sure enough, a few weeks later she had a dream in which her girlfriend was in the water, and the sharks were going to get her. She dived in and saved her — perfectly safe. She was able to move from being killed by the shark, to being bitten by the shark, to then actually confronting it and dealing with it."

In Your Child's Dreams, Garfield spent a lot of time talking to parents about what to do when the child has nightmares, which must be an issue, for practically every parent. It's an ancient technique. All the old cultures had ways of dealing with dreams.Some of the ancient methods seem to still work. "I think that now it would be hard for a kid to accept that, but what we can do that's just as effective, is tell them, "GI Joe will come."

You can have anything you want happen in it. You could get somebody strong to help you. Who do you know who's strong? Parents who talk with a child in this way are able to change the child's nightmares. For instance, one of my friends, Mary, her little boy Richard was having terrible nightmares about a lion chasing him. I discussed this method, and she said, "I'm going to try that, because I usually have to stay up for an hour, patting his back and telling him to think happy thoughts, and so forth. So she said to him, the next time he had the nightmare about the lion, "Richard, you know, this is your dream. You can have anything you want happen in it. You could get somebody who's strong help you. Who could you get? Who do you know who's strong?" And he said, "How about Ultra Man? Could I get Ultra Man?" She said, "Sure, it's your dream. You can have anybody you want, anything you want, happen." She said he lay right back down on the pillow, his eyes all round. He couldn't wait to go back to sleep."

This is a very profound notion. I mean, it's not just childish to say, "It's your dream." And when the child learns that, or the dreamer of any age, it is not just the dream that changes. You are teaching a lesson in living, because it carries over. You're saying to the child, "You can do something about your life. You don't have to be a passive victim. You can be an active participant. You've got your choice. You've got options. You can do something to make your life different." So it's not just the dream that changes. It is powerful.

A lot of Garfield's more recent work involves looking at the human life cycle — particularly the human life cycle of females, in her most recent book — in showing how dreams serve almost like rites of passage, or as landmarks, as we move through important phases in the life cycle.

In our society we don't have rites of passage for the most part. We have weddings, but we very seldom celebrate a girl's menarche, her first menstruation. We certainly don't celebrate a woman's menopause, which is the equivalent kind of happening. And retiring. You know, different stages of life are very seldom recognized, other than getting married and having babies, which are generally accepted as joyful occasions. But in our dream life we are marking those events very powerfully, and they can, if we pay attention to them, help us to integrate the events. So although the dreams do belong to us, they also in a way serve as a teacher. There's a value in some sense to being the passive observer of a dream from time to time. Our dreams can teach us, even if we don't pay attention or work with them actively. They've got something to say — that unopened letter — if you can learn to read the letter. It's very important, of course, to understand the language of the dream. I think of it as a kind of set of hieroglyphs, and if you understand the pictures, then you can read that message. You can make a kind of translation of your dream.

First of all you need to write your dreams down. You need to keep track of them, keep a diary. Ask yourself questions about the images in the dream, if they're not apparent to you. You might know, "That dog with a shaggy haircut, that sort of poodle haircut, that's just like Joe at the office who's giving me a hard time. He has hair that looks sort of like a poodle."

You begin to elaborate in your own mind on the dream images. The meanings become more apparent. But even more specifically you can say, "Who is Joe?" Maybe Joe was in the dream himself. What kind of person is he? And try to describe a character or a thing in your dream, in a way that a person who doesn't know them can understand them. For instance, the dreamer might say, "Oh, Joe is a really difficult guy. He's always judging people. He's always making these critical judgments." OK, if Joe is in your dream, it can be that you're being annoyed with this critical person, but it also can be the Joe within you, the critical part of yourself which is symbolized by this external person. And you begin to understand that the people in your dreams may represent themselves, and sometimes they do. They often represent a part of you.

Certain Gestalt people say that every image in a dream represents a part of you. And we can always learn something from looking at our dreams in that way. If this is a part of me, if that red bug is me, and talking for the red bug, what does it have to say? What do I need to hear from that? But dreams also do something more. They're not always about our immediate problems, and the immediate things that are going on in our lives. They sometimes tell us about the future. It's more rare, but there also is an aspect of dreaming that is beyond the ordinary understanding. "I've gotten some of my best ideas in dreams. Even the title of a book, for example. I had named Your Child's Dreams, Dream Child, which I liked better. It was very poetic, and I enjoyed it. Too poetic, said my publisher; come up with something else. And I looked back in my dream diary, and I saw that the night I decided to call it Dream Child, I had had a dream in which a woman said to me, "Well, I would have called it Your Child's Dreams." And at the time I thought, "Well, that's sort of interesting, but I like Dream Child better," and I stuck to it. But when my editor said, "You have to come up with a different title; this isn't going to work. It could be poetry, it could be a novel. Come up with something that has dream in it, and children in it." So I made up a list of about ten different names over the weekend, and I just put the dream name in among them, and on Monday morning I called her and said, "Here's my list. What do you think sounds best?" I read the list of names. She said, "Your Child's Dreams. That's it. That's perfect." And it was the dream name."

Someone else had a tough time teaching his son maths. Then one evening he had a dream. In the dream he was at a resort with his son, and heard this song they were singing, and it went "You can't remember the words to this song, because you make them up as you go along." And he got up the next morning, and began telling his to make up rhymes to go with his math. So he got into it, and he went "Six times seven is forty-two; if you don't believe me, I'll kiss your shoe." And he got right through his multiplication tables that way. The dream really gave him the answer.

Whatever their problems are, whatever they're coping with, they've got some of the answer inside, if they just listen. One would almost think that if our dreams really can reveal the future — and there's quite a bit of research now that suggests that — then really there should be no problem that a dream would be incapable of solving, if we look.

There certainly is a lot going on in there that we haven't paid enough attention to, and I think it's really important to listen to our dreams, because they're talking to us.

■ ■ ■

25

PATANJALI

HEALING THROUGH YOGA

The Yoga Therapy or ' yoga-chikitsa' refers to the treatment of diseases by means of yogic exercises which may be physical or mental or both. It is a specialised form of yogic culture. This mode of treatment has been practised in India from very ancient times. Many references to yoga have been made in the Upanishads. It was, however, Maharishi Patanjali who in about the first century B.C. gave a systematic account of the traditional yogic teaching. Later other sages built on it. The term ' Yoga' is derived from the Sanskrit root 'yug' which means "to join" It signifies union between the individual soul (jivatma) and the universal soul (parmatma). It aims at obtaining relief from pain and suffering. Basically, human evolution takes place on three different planes, namely physical, mental and spiritual. Yoga is a means of attaining perfect health by maintaining harmony and achieving optimum functioning on all three levels through complete self-control.

Yogic kriyas, asanas and pranayama constitute the physical basis of yoga. The practice of kriyas and asanas leads to excellent circulation. It also energises and stimulates major endocrine glands of the body. Yogic exercises promote inner health and harmony, and their regular practice helps prevent and cure many common ailments. They also help eliminate tensions, be they physical, mental or emotional.Pranayama slows down the ageing process. In ordinary respiration, one breathes roughly 15 times a minute, taking in approximately 20 cubic inches of air. In pranayama the breathing rate is slowed down to once or twice a minute and the breath inhaled is deep and full, taking nearly 100 cubic inches of air.All yogic exercises should be performed on a clean mat, a carpet or a blanket covered with a cotton sheet. Clothing should be light and loose-fitting to allow free movement of the limbs. The mind should be kept off all disturbances and tensions. Regularity and punctuality in practising yogic exercises is essential. Generally, 5 a.m. to 8 a.m. is the ideal time for yoga practices.

Yoga asanas and pranayama should be practised only after mastering the techniques with the help of a competent teacher. Asanas should always be practised on an empty stomach. Shavasana should be practised for a brief period before starting the rest of the exercises as this will create the right mental condition. Asanas should be performed at a leisurely slow-motion pace, maintaining poise and balance.Herein are described certain yogic kriyas, asanas and pranayama which have specific therapeutic values and are highly beneficial in the maintenance of health and the healing of diseases.

Kriyas: A disease-free system should be the starting ground for yogasanas and pranayama. There are six specific cleansing techniques, known as Shat Kriyas, which eliminate impurities and help cure many ailments. Of these, the following four can be practised safely.

Jalaneti: Most diseases of the nose and throat are caused by the accumulation of impurities in the nasal passage. Jalaneti is a process of cleansing the air passage of the nostrils and the throat by washing them with tepid saline water. Take a clean jalaneti pot. Put half a teaspoonful of salt in the pot and fill it with lukewarm drinking water. Stand up and tilt your head slightly to the right. Insert the nozzle of the pot in the left nostril and let the water flow into it. Inhale and exhale through the mouth, allowing the water to flow out through the right nostril. Reverse this process by tilting your head to the left and letting the water flow from the right to the left nostril. Jalaneti should be practised only in the morning. It will relieve sore throat, cold, cough, sinusitis, migraine, headache and cases of inflammation of the nasal membranes. It keeps the head cool and improves vision.

Vamana Dhouti or Kunjal: This is a process of cleansing the interior of the stomach. Drink four to six glasses of tepid water, with a little salt added to it, early in the morning on an empty stomach. Then stand up, bend forward, insert the middle and index fingers of the right hand into the mouth until they touch the uvulva. Tickle it until you feel a vomiting sensation. The saline water thus ejected will bring up bile and other toxic matter with it. Repeat the process till all the water is vomited out. This should be done once a week or as and when necessary.It is beneficial for cleansing the stomach in cases of excessive bile, constipation, and gastric troubles. Persons suffering from hyperacidity should perform kunjal with unsalted water. It gives relief from headaches, nervous weakness, chronic cold, cough and asthma. It should not be practised by those suffering from high blood pressure, ulcers and heart trouble. Kapalbhati : Kapala means 'skull' and bhati means 'shine'. This is a respiratory exercise for the abdomen and diaphragm. The channels inside the nose and other parts of the respiratory system are purified by this exercise. In the process, the brain is also cleared.

Sit in a comfortable position, preferably in padmasana. Exercise the diaphragm by exhaling suddenly and quickly through both nostrils, producing a hissing sound. Inhaling will be automotive and passive. The air should be exhaled from the lungs with a sudden, vigorous inward stroke of the front abdominal muscles. The abdominal stroke should be complete and the breath should be expelled fully. While inhaling, no willful expansion is necessary and the abdominal muscles should be relaxed. This exercise should be done in three phases, each consisting of 20 to 30 strokes a minute. A little rest can be taken in between . Throughout, the thoracic muscles should be kept contracted. Kapalbhati enables the inhalation of a good amount of oxygen which purifies the blood and strengthens the nerve and brain centres. This kriya provides relief in many lung, throat and chest diseases like chronic bronchitis, asthma, pleurisy and tuberculosis.

Trataka: In yoga, four exercises have been prescribed for strengthening weak eye muscles, relieving eye strain and curing of eye disease. They are known as ' Trataka ' ,which in sanskrit means Winkles gaze at a particular point." or looking at an object with awareness. The four tratakas are : Dakshinay jatru trataka in which, with face forwards, the eyes are fixed on the tip of the right shoulder; Vamajatru trataka, in which the eyes are fixed on the tip of the left shoulder ; Namikagra trataka, in which the eyes are focussed on the tip of the nose, and Bhrumadhya trataka, in which the eyes are focussed on the space between the eyebrows. These exercises should be practiced from a meditative position like padmasana or vajrasana. The gaze should be maintained for as long as you are comfortable, gradually increasing the period from 10 to 20 and then to 30 seconds. The eyes should be closed and rested after each exercise. Persons with acute myopia should perform the tratakas wit h their eyes closed.

Asanas: Shavasana (Dead body pose)

Lie flat on your back, feet comfortably part, arms and hands extended about six inches from the body, palms upwards and fingers half-folded. Close your eyes. Begin by consciously and gradually relaxing every part and each muscle of the body ; feet, legs, calves, knees, thighs, abdomen, hips, back, hands, arms, chest, shoulders, neck, head and face. Relax yourself completely feeling as if your whole body is lifeless. Now concentrate your mind on breathing rhythmically as slowly and effortlessly as possible. This creates a state of complete relaxation. Remain motionless in this position, relinquishing all responsibilities and worries for 10 to 15 minutes.

Discontinue the exercise when your legs grow numb. This asana helps bring down high blood pressure, and relieves the mind, particularly for those who are engaged in excessive mental activity. This exercise should be done both at the beginning and at the end of the daily round of yogic asanas.

During a fast, shavasana soothes the nervous system.

Padmasana (Lotus pose)

Sit erect and stretch your legs out in front of you. Bend one leg to place the foot on the thigh of the other, the sole facing upwards. Similarly, bend the other leg too, so that the heels are opposite each other and placed in such a way that they press down on the other side of the groin. Keep your neck, head and spine straight. Place your palms one upon the other, both turned upward and cupped, and rest them on the upturned heels a little below the navel.

Padmasana is a good pose for doing pranayama and meditation. It helps in the treatment of many heart and lung diseases and digestive disorders. It also calms and refreshes the mind.

Yogamudra : Sit erect in padmasana. Fold your hands behind your back, holding your left wrist with the right hand. Take a deep breath. While exhaling, bend forward slowly keeping your hands on your back. Bring your face downwards until your nose and forehead touch the floor. While inhaling , slowly rise back to the upright position. The practice of this asana tones up the nervous system, builds up powerful abdominal muscles and strengthens the pelvic organs. It helps pep up digestion, boosts the appetite and removes constipation. It tones up and relaxes the nerves of the head and face. It also strengthens the sex glands.

Vajrasana (Pelvic pose)

Sit erect and stretch out your legs. Fold your legs back, placing the feet on the sides of the buttocks with the soles facing back and upwards. Rest your buttocks on the floor between your heels. The toes of both feet should touch. Now, place your hands on your knees and keep the spine, neck and head straight. Vajrasana can be performed even after meals. It improves the digestion and is beneficial in cases of dyspepsia, constipation, colitis, seminal weakness and stiffness of the legs. It strengthens the hips, thighs, knees, calves, ankles and toes.

Shirshasana (Topsy turvy pose)

Shirsha means ' head ' . In this asana, one stands on one's head. Kneel on the ground, interlocking the fingers of both hands. Place the ' fingerlock ' on the ground in front of you, keeping the elbows apart. Support your head on the fingerlock. Start raising your knees one at a time, to chest level. Then raise your feet slowly so that the calf muscles touch the thighs. Breathe normally. This is the first stage which should be done perfectly as the balance of the final posture depends mainly on this stage. Next, raise your knees first and then slowly raise the feet so that the whole body is straight, like a pillar. This is the final pose. Return to the original position by reversing the order, step by step. This asana should not be done jerkily. The important factor in shirshasana is mastering the balance, which comes through gradual practice. For proper balance, elbows should be placed firmly on the ground, alongside the fingerlock. Initially the asana should be done for 60 seconds only. The duration may be gradually increased by a further 10 seconds each week.Regular practice of shirshasana will benefit the nervous, circulatory, respiratory, digestive, excretory and endocrine systems. This asana helps cases of dyspepsia, seminal weakness, varicose veins, arteriosclerosis, jaundice, renal colic and congested liver. Those suffering from oozing from the ears, iritis, high blood pressure or a weak heart should not practice this asana.

Viparitakarani (Inverted action pose)

Lie flat on your back, with your feet together and arms by your side. Press your palms down, raising your legs to a perpendicular position without bending the knees. Your palms should touch the waist. Then straighten your legs. The trunk should not make a right angle with the ground but simply an upward slanting position. The chest should not press against the chin but be kept a little away. To return to the ground, bring your legs down slowly, evenly balancing your weight.Through this asana, the muscles of the neck become stronger and blood circulation is improved. The functioning of the cervical nerves, ganglia and the thyroid also gets improved.

Sarvagasana (Shoulder stand pose)

In Sanskrit 'sarva' means whole and 'anga' means limb. Almost all parts of the body are involved in and benefit from this asana. Lie flat on your back with your arms by the side, palms turned down. Bring your legs up slowly to a 90 o angle and then raise the rest of the body by pushing the legs up and resting their raise the rest of the body by pushing the legs up and resting their weight on the arms. Fix your chin in jugular notch, and use your arms and hands to support the body at the hip region. The weight of the body should rest on your head, back and shoulders, your arms being used merely for balance. The trunk and legs should be in a straight line. The body, legs , hips and trunk should be kept as vertical as possible. Focus your eyes on your big toes. Press your chin against your chest. Hold the pose for one to three minutes. Return to the starting position slowly reversing the procedure.Sarvangasana helps relieve bronchitis, dyspepsia, varicose veins and peps up the digestion. It stimulates the thyroid and para-thyroid glands, influences the bran, heart and lungs. It helps lymphatic juices to circulate in the brain and strengthens the mind. This asana should not be done by those suffering Viparitkarani from high blood pressure, heart disease and eye trouble.

Matsyasana (Fish pose)

Sit in padmasana. Bend backwards and lie flat on your back without raising your knees. Press your palms beneath the shoulder. Push the hip backwards thus making a bridge -like arch with the spine. Then making hooks of your forefingers, grasp your toes without crossing your arms. Maintain this pose and breathe rhythmically and comfortably. Reverse the order and return gradually to the starting position of Padamasana. Matsyasana is beneficial in the treatment of acidity, constipation, diabetes, asthma, bronchitis and other lung disorders.

Uttanapadasana (Left-lifting pose)

Lie on your back with leg and arms straight, feet together, palms facing downwards, on the floor close to the body. Raise your legs above two feet from the floor without bending your knees. Maintain this pose for some time. Then, lower your legs slowly without bending the knees. This asana is helpful for those suffering from constipation. It strengthens the abdominal muscles and intestinal organs.

Halasana (Plough pose)

Lie flat on your back with legs and feet together, arms by your side with fists closed near your thigh keeping your legs straight, slowly raise them to angles of 300, 600 and 900, pausing slightly at each point. Gradually, raise your legs above your head without bending your knees and then move them behind until they touch the floor. Stretch your legs as far as possible so that your chin presses tightly against the chest while your arms remain on the floor as in the original position. Hold the pose from between 10 seconds to three minutes, breathing normally. To return to the starting position slowly reverse the procedure.

This asana relieves tension in the back, neck, and legs and is beneficial in the treatment of lumbago, spinal rigidity and rheumatism, myalgia, arthritis, sciatics and asthma.

Bhujangasana (Cobra pose)

Lie on your stomach with your legs straight and feet together, toes pointing backwards. Rest your forehead and nose on the ground. Place your palms below the shoulders and your arms by the side of the chest. Inhale and slowly raise your head, neck, chest and upper abdomen from the navel up. Bend your spine back and arch your back as far as you can looking upwards. Maintain this position and hold your breathe for a few seconds. Exhale, and slowly return to the original position. This asana has great therapeutic value in the treatment of diseases like cervical spondylitis, bronchitis, asthma and eosinophillia. It removes weakness of the abdomen and tones up the reproductive system in women. It exercises the vertebrae, back muscles and the spine.

Shalabhasana (Locust pose)

Lie flat on your stomach, with your legs stretched out straight, feet together, chin and nose resting on the ground, looking straight ahead. Move your arms under the body, keeping them straight, fold your hands into fists and place them close to the thighs. Now, raise your legs up keeping them straight together and stretching them as far back as possible without bending your knees and toes. Hold this position for a few seconds and repeat four or five times. This asana helps in the treatment of arthritis, rheumatism and low backache. The whole body is strengthened by this asana especially the waist, chest, back and neck. Persons suffering from high blood pressure or heart disease should not practice this asana.

Dhanurasana (Bow pose)

Lie on your stomach with your chin resting on the ground, arms extended alongside the body with the legs straight. Bend your legs back towards the hips, bring them forward and grasp your ankles. Inhale and raise your thighs, chest and head at the same time. Keep your hands straight. The weight of the body should rest mainly on the navel region. Therefore, arch your spine as much as possible. Exhale and return slowly to the starting position, by reversing the procedure.

Dhanurasana provides good exercise for the arms, shoulders, legs, ankles, back and neck. It also strengthens the spine. It relieves flatulence and constipation and improves the functioning of the pancreas and the intestines. It should not be done by those with a weak heart, high blood pressure and ulcers of the stomach and bowels.

Makarasana (Crocodile pose)

Lie flat on your abdomen. Spread your legs, with heels pointing towards each other. Bring your left hand under the right shoulder and grasp it. Grasp the left shoulder with your right hand, keeping the elbows together, one upon the other on the ground. Your face should be between your crossed hands. Relax and breathe normally for two or three minutes. Then gradually go back to the sitting position.

This asana completely relaxes both the body and the mind and also rests the muscles. It is beneficial in the treatment of hypertension, heart disease and mental disorders. Vakrasana : Sit erect and stretch legs out. Raise your right knee until your foot rests by the side of the left knee. Place your right hand behind your back without twisting the trunk too much. Then bring your left arm from in front of you over the right knee. Place your left palm on the ground near the heel of your right foot. Push your knee as far as to the left arm. Twist your trunk to the right as much as possible. Turn your face to the right over the right shoulder. Release and repeat on the left side.

This asana tones up the spinal and abdominal muscles and nerves and activates the kidneys, intestines, stomach, adrenaline and gonad glands. It relieves cases of constipation and dyspepsia.

Ardhamatsyendrasana

This is the half position of Matsyendrasana, which is named after the great sage Matsyendra. Sit erect on the ground, stretching your legs in front of you. Insert your left heel in the perineum, keeping the left thigh straight. Place your right foot flat on the floor, crossing the left knee. Pass your left arm over the right knee and grasp the big toe of your right foot. Grasp your left thigh from the rear with your right hand. Turn your head, neck, shoulders and trunk to the right bringing your chin in line with the right shoulder. Maintain this position for a few seconds, gradually increasing the duration to 2 minutes. Repeat the same process on the other side for the same duration.

This asana exercises the vertebrae and keeps them in good shape. It helps the liver, spleen, bladder, pancreas, intestines and other abdominal organs, and also stretches and strengthens the spinal nerves. This asana is beneficial in the treatment of obesity, dyspepsia, asthma and diabetes.

Paschimottanasana (Posterior stretching pose)

Sit erect. Stretch your legs out in front of you, keeping them close to each other. Bend your trunk and head forward from the waist without bending your knees and grasp the big toes with your rest your forehead on your knees. With practice, the tense muscles become supple enough for this exercise. Old persons and persons whose spine is still should do this asana slowly in the initial stages. The final pose need be maintained only for a few seconds. Return to the starting position gradually.

Paschimottanasana is a good stretching exercise in which the posterior muscles get stretched and relaxed. It relieves sciatica, muscular rheumatism of the back, backache, lumbago and asthmatic attacks. It is also valuable in constipation, dyspepdis and other abdominal disorders.

Gomukhasana (Cow-face pose)

Sit erect on the floor, with your legs outstretched. Fold your leg back. Place your left foot under the right hip. Similarly, fold back the right leg and cross your right foot over your left thigh. Place your right heel against the left hip. Both soles should face backwards, one over the other. Now interlock your hands behind your back. See to it that if your right leg is over the left, then your right elbow should face upward and the left elbow downward. This position is reversed when the leg position is changed. Hold the pose for 30 seconds and then repeat the procedure reversing the process. The practice of gomukhasana will strengthen the muscles of the upper arm, shoulder, chest, back, waist and thigh. It is beneficial in the treatment of seminal weakness, piles, urethral disorders and kidney troubles. It also relieves varicose veins and sciatica.

Pavanmuktasana (Gas-releasing pose)

Lie flat on your back, hands by your side. Fold your legs back, placing your feet flat on the floor ; make a fingerlock with your hands and place them a little below the knees. Bring your thighs up near your chest. Exhale and raise your head and shoulders and bring your nose between your knees. This is the final position. Maintain this pose for a few seconds and repeat three to five times. Reverse the procedure to get back to the original position.

This asana strengthens the abdominal muscles and internal abdominal organs like the liver, spleen, pancreas and stomach. It helps release excessive gas from the abdomen and relieves flatulence. Persons suffering from constipation should do this exercise in the morning after drinking lukewarm water to help proper evacuation of the bowels.

Chakrasana (Lateral bending pose)

Stand straight with your feet and toes together and arms by your sides, palms facing and touching the thighs. Raise one arm laterally above the head with the palm inwards up to shoulder level and palm upwards when the arm rises above the level of your head. Then, bend your trunk and head sideways with the raised arm touching the ear, and sliding the palm of the other hand downwards towards the knee. Keep your knees and elbows straight throughout. Maintain the final pose for a few seconds. Then gradually bring your hand back to the normal position. Repeat the exercise on the other side.

This asana induces maximum stretching of the lateral muscles of the body, especially the abdomen. It strengthens the knees, arms and shoulders and increases lung capacity.

Trikonasana (Triangle pose)

Stand erect, with your legs apart. Stretch your arms up to shoulder level. Bend your trunk forwards and twist to the left, looking upwards and keeping your left arm raised at an angle of 90 degrees. Place your right palm on your left foot without bending the knees. Maintain this pose for a few seconds. Then straighten up and return to the normal position. Repeat the procedure on the other side.

Trikosnaana is an all-round stretching exercise. It keeps the spinal column flexible and reduces the fat on the lateral sides of the body. Besides, it stimulates the adrenal glands and tones up the abdominal and pelvic organs.

Pranayama

Prana means 'vital force' and Ayama means 'control' in Sanskrit. Thus Pranayama means the control of the vital force through concentration and regulated breathing. By means of controlled breathing that is, inhaling and exhaling by holding the breath for a fixed time and changing the rhythm of inspiration and expiration, it is possible to influence the life-force in the body. Pranayama is the process by which such conscious control is achieved through controlled and rhythmical breathing. Pranayama purifies the channels along which the life stream of 'prana' flows in the body and prevents various disorders. It increases one's resistance to respiratory diseases.

The best position in which to practice pranayama is the padmasana or lotus pose. If for some reason that position is difficult to adopt, it can be done while sitting in any comfortable pose. The important thing is to keep the back, neck and head in a straight line. The body should be in its natural relaxed condition and this can be achieved by resting a few minutes in shavasan. If necessary, use your right finger and thumb on either side of the nose to control the right and left nostrils during inhalation and exhalation. In practising pranayama, a ratio of two to one should be maintained throughout, that is, the exhalation time should be double that required for inhalation. For instance, if inhalation takes 5 seconds, exhalation should take 10 seconds. Both inhalation and exhalation should be smooth and quiet. Some varieties of pranayama beneficial in the treatment of common ailments are as follows :

Anuloma-viloma: This is also known as Nadishuddhi pranayama. Sit in any comfortable meditative pose, keeping your head, neck and spine erect. Rest your left hand on your left knee. Close your right nostril by pressing the tip of your right thumb against it.

Breathe out slowly through the left nostril. Inhale slowly and deeply through the left nostril, keeping the right nostril closed. Close your left nostril with the little finger and ring finger of your right hand and exhale through the right nostril. Then inhale through the right nostril, keeping the left nostril closed and, lastly, exhale through the left nostril, keeping the right nostril closed. This completes one round of anuloma-viloma. Repeat the entire process. Inhaling and exhaling should be done very slowly, without making any sound.

This pranayama is a process of purification. It strengthens the lungs and calms the nerves. It helps cure cough and cold, insomnia, chronic headache and asthma.

Ujjayi: Sit in any comfortable meditative pose. Inhale slowly, deeply and steadily through both nostrils with a low uniform sound through the glottis. Hold your breathe for a second or two after inhaling and then exhale noisily only through the left nostril, keeping the right nostril closed. Do this as often as required. This pranayama clears the nasal passage and helps the functioning of the thyroid gland and benefits respiratory disorders, especially bronchitis and asthma. Persons suffering from high blood pressure should not practice ujjayi.

Bhastrika: 'Bhastrika' means 'bellows.' It is performed by instant and quick expirations of breath. There are many varieties of bhastrika. The simplest technique is as follows : Sit in padmasana. Do 20 strokes of kapalbhati. Inhale and exhale rapidly, making a puffing sound. This is a good exercise for abdominal viscera and lungs.

Sheetali: Sit in padamasana or any other comfortable posture. Stick your tongue out about an inche from the lips, rolled up at the sides to form a channel like a bird's beak. Suck in air through the channel. After a full inhalation, slowly close your mouth, hold your breath and exhale slowly through both nostrils. This completes the exercise. Repeat as required. This pranayama cools the body and mind, activates the liver and bile and has beneficial effects on the circulation and body temperature.

Sitkari: In sitkari a sound is produced while inhaling by opening the mouth a little, placing the tip of the tongue against the lower front teeth and then sucking the air in slowly. After holding your breath, exhale through both nostrils. This exercise helps to control thirst, hunger and laziness.

Suryabhedan: 'Surya-nadi ' is the right nostril and ' ChandraNadi' is the left nostril. In this pranayama, one always uses the right nostril for inhalation. Sit in padmasan or any other suitable posture. Keep your head, neck and back straight. Inhale through the right nostril. Hold your breath and then exhale through the left nostril. Hold your breath and then exhale through the left nostril. Repeat as often as required. This pranayama increases gastric juices and helps digestion. It also fortifies the nervous system and clears the sinuses.

Bhramari: In this pranayama, the buzzing sound of a bee is produced and hence it is called bhramari. Keep your mouth closed while inhaling. Exhale through both nostrils, producing the humming sound of a bee. This pranayama affects the ears, nose, eyes and mouth and makes the complexion glow. It also helps those suffering from insomnia.

■ ■ ■

26

Rosemary Gladstar

HERBAL HEALING

Rosemary Gladstar is the founder of The California School of Herbal Studies (based in Forestville, California), United Plant Savers, and co-founder of Sage Mountain Herbs. She is also the original owner of Rosemary's Garden in Sebastopol, CA. The author of several books including the popular Herbal Healing For Women, she has taught herbology extensively through out the U.S. and led traveladventurers to study Third World medicine in many parts of the globe. Her experience includes over 20 years in the herbal community as a healer, teacher, visionary and organizer of large herbal events. She currently resides in Vermont.

Rosemary Gladstar comes from a family of herbalists. Her grandmother had a profound influence on her when she was growing up. She never formally called herself an herbalist, but she was very aware of the plants. Like many people of her generation, she used plants as part of her lifestyle. Her grandparents came to America during the Turkish invasion of Armenia. They had been on the Death March and they had escaped. Her grandmother always credited their survival to their belief in God and to her knowledge of the plants. So she had a greater reason for wanting her children and grandchildren to know the plants. She didn't do formal training, she didn't say, "Now we're doing an herb class." But she would go out and pick the plants. Rosemary Gladstar's parents were farmers and they knew the plants. It was part of their lifestyle. She always likes to go back to those roots because that's how she wants people to use plants–not as a system of medicine but as a system of life, part of our heritage as humans.

Using plants is traditional–it goes back before formal education. "One of the things I see happening is we've pigeon-holed herbs into a medical system and they're really far more about life, than they are about a system of healing. They're about vitality and joy and daily living. So that's been one of my missions in my whole career as an herbalist–trying to bring plants back into a living modality, as part of a lifestyle and not limited to the medical system, not waiting to use them until you need them for medicinal reasons, but using them as part of your preventive lifestyle along with healthy foods."

Gladstar believes they can teach us how to live better here on this planet. Watching how plants live and how they give of themselves, how they give back to the rest of the community that we live in, the plant and animal kingdoms. The herb store came about mostly as a dream of hers, giving the earth back to the people. It was at a time when herbs weren't readily available. There was no herb store in Northern California. There was one old one in San Francisco that was a tremendous model, but there were no other herb stores. At that time Chinese herbalism wasn't what it is now, when it's readily available to people. Actually, oftentimes when you went to Chinatown they wouldn't even speak English to you, so you didn't have the same type of accessibility to Chinese herbalists that you have now, Gladstar recalls. "I didn't even really envision a store, more like a home dispensary that people could come to, you know, they could just come up to my house. It was in Monte Rio at that time, but I ended up not opening a store in my house because I lived up on the end of this very windy road. There was a little store called the Guerneville Natural Foods Store. They had a little closet there, and I asked if I could rent it. That was the first Rosemary's Garden, a little corner of the store. Eventually it took over half of the store, and then moved over to its own location."

Gladstar lives on a mountain, surrounded by thousands and thousands of acres of wilderness. That's where Sage Mountain Retreat Center & Botanical Sanctuary is located. She created a nature center here, for growing and preserving the heirloom plants. When she moved to Vermont, I was very remote; there wasn't a lot of community around there. And living in the wilderness she became critically aware of the status of the plants themselves. She began to recognize that though herbalism was experiencing a tremendous renaissance and becoming very popular, none of us were really focusing on the status of the plants. We weren't really addressing the facts about how the plants were doing in populations and what the impact of our harvesting was. There really weren't any long term studies of growing and harvesting plants, and what it would be like 50 or 100 years from now. So she came to this piece of property, that was wilderness, where so many of valuable plants originate from. A lot of the plants that are used in North American medicine are from the Southeast and Northeast. This is their native habitat. And they were not available in large amounts at all. She said, "Why don't we form an organization, where we can really bring awareness to the issue?" She started a very small grass roots organization called United Plant Savers (UpS), six years ago. And 70 or 80% of her time goes into this organization. "It's all non-profit work, but it's been so gratifying and it's made a big difference. Organic cultivation is being looked at on a much higher level, as an alternative to wildcrafting herbs from their dwindling native habitats. UpS creates a lot of controversy, because we don't have absolute answers. We don't want to create hysteria, but we want to be cautious until we get the actual figures from scientific studies."

In 2001 Gladstar bought a 370 acre botanical preserve in Ohio that is incredibly rich. The native species were never harvested or logged. There are acres and acres of indigenous goldenseal, for example. She is turning it into a permanent Botanical Sanctuary for future generations of herbalists. It's the first of it's kind in the country.

"We're trying to provide a forum for the questions. We have a Board of Directors comprised of big and small businesses, practitioners, folklore and herbalists, wildcrafters, so that all aspects are represented. We need to recognize that this is a problem, and that if we don't address it, we are going to be in a dangerous situation as far as these plants go. Our goal is to safeguard the herbs. They're not just here for our use. They're here for their own integrity as part of the environment."

One of the things that is important is to create work for yourself that is meaningful, that involves you in the positive. That makes all the difference in the world.

■ ■ ■

27

VINCENT PRIESSNITZ

HEALING THROUGH NATURE

Nature cure is a constructive method of treatment which aims at removing the basic cause of disease through the rational use of the elements freely available in nature. It is not only a system of healing, but also a way of life, in tune with the internal vital forces or natural elements comprising the human body. It is a complete revolution in the art and science of living. Although the term ' naturopathy' is of relatively recent origin, the philosophical basis and several of the methods of nature cure treatments are ancient. It was practised in ancient Egypt, Greece and Rome. Hippocrates, the father of medicine (460-357 B.C.) strongly advocated it. India, it appears, was much further advanced in older days in natural healing system than other countries of the world. There are references in India's ancient sacred books about the extensive use of nature's excellent healing agents such as air, earth, water and sun. The Great Baths of the Indus Valley civilisation as discovered at Mohenjodaro in old Sind testifies to the use of water for curative purposes in ancient India.The modern methods of nature cure originated in Germany in 1822, when Vincent Priessnitz established the first hydropathic establishment there. With his great success in water cure, the idea of drugless healing spread throughout the civilised world and many medical practitioners throughout the civilised world and many medical practitioncrs from America and other countries became his enthusiastic students and disciples. These students subsequently enlarged and developed the various methods of natural healing in their own way. The whole mass of knowledge was later collected under one name, Naturopathy.

The credit for the name Naturopathy goes to Dr. Benedict Lust (1872 - 1945), and hence he is called the Father of Naturopathy. Nature cure is based on the realisation that man is born healthy and strong and that he can stay as such as living in accordance with the laws of nature. Even if born with some inherited affliction, the individual can eliminate it by putting to the best use the natural agents of healing. Fresh air, sunshine, a proper diet, exercise, scientific relaxation, constructive thinking and the right mental attitude, along with prayer and meditation all play their part in keeping a sound mind in a sound body.

Nature cure believes that disease is an abnormal condition of the body resulting from the violation of the natural laws. Every such violation has repercussions on the human system in the shape of lowered vitality, irregularities of the blood and lymph and the accumulation of waste matter and toxins. Thus, through a faulty diet it is not the digestive system alone which is adversely affected. When toxins accumulate, other organs such as the bowels, kidneys, skin and lungs are overworked and cannot get rid of these harmful substances as quickly as they are produced. Besides this, mental and emotional disturbances cause imbalances of the vital electric field within which cell metabolism takes place, producing toxins. When the soil of this electric filed is undisturbed, disease-causing germs can live in it without multiplying or producing toxins. It is only when it is disturbed or when the blood is polluted with toxic waste that the germs multiply and become harmful.

Basic Principles: The whole philosophy and practice of nature cure is built on three basic principles. These principles are based on the conclusions reached from over a century of effective naturopathic treatment of diseases in Germany, America and Great Britain. They have been tested and proved over and over again by the results obtained. The first and most basic principle of nature cure is that all forms of disease are due to the same cause, namely, the accumulations of waste materials and bodily refuse in the system. These waste materials in the healthy individual are removed from the system through the organs of elimination. But in the diseased person, they are steadily piling up in the body through years of faulty habits of living such as wrong feeding, improper care of the body and habits contributing to enervation and nervous exhaustion such as worry, overwork and excesses of all kinds. It follows from this basic principle that the only way to cure disease is to employ methods which will enable the system to throw off these toxic accumulations.

All natural treatments are actually directed towards this end.

The second basic principle of nature cure is that all acute diseases such as fevers, colds, inflammations, digestive disturbances and skin eruptions are nothing more than self-initiated efforts on the part of the body to throw off the accumulated waste materials and that all chronic diseases such as heart disease, diabetes, rheumatism, asthma, kidney disorders, are the results of continued suppression of the acute diseases through harmful methods such as drugs, vaccines, narcotics and gland extracts.

The third principle of nature cure is that the body contains an elaborate healing mechanism which has the power to bring about a return to normal condition of health, provided right methods are employed to enable it to do so. In other words, the power to cure disease lies within the body itself and not in the hands of the doctor.

Nature Cure vs Modern System: The modern medical system treats the symptoms and suppresses the disease but does little to ascertain the real cause. Toxic drugs which may suppress or relieve some ailments usually have harmful side-effects. Drugs usually hinder the self-healing efforts of the body and make recovery more difficult. According to the late Sir William Osler, an eminent physician and surgeon, when drugs are used, the patient has to recover twice - once from the illness, and once from the drug. Drugs cannot cure diseases; disease continues. It is only its pattern that changes. Drugs also produce dietary deficiencies by destroying nutrients, using them up, and preventing their absorption. Moreover, the toxicity they produce occurs at a time when the body is least capable of coping with it. The power to restore health thus lies not in drugs, but in nature.

The approach of modern system is more on combative lines after the disease has set in, whereas nature cure system lays greater emphasis on preventive method and adopts measures to attain and maintain health and prevent disease. The modern medical system treats each disease as a separate entity, requiring specific drug for its cure, whereas the nature cure system treats the organism as a whole and seeks to restore harmony to the whole of the patient's being.

Methods of Nature Cure: The nature cure system aims at the readjustment of the human system from abnormal to normal conditions and functions, and adopts methods of cure which are in conformity with the constructive principles of nature. Such methods remove from the system the accumulation of toxic matter and poisons without in any way injuring the vital organs of the body. They also stimulate the organs of elimination and purification to better functioning.

To cure disease, the first and foremost requirement is to regulate the diet. To get rid of accumulated toxins and restore the equilibrium of the system, it is desirable to completely exclude acid-forming foods, including proteins, starches and fats, for a week or more and to confine the diet to fresh fruits which will disinfect the stomach and alimentary canal. If the body is overloaded with morbid matter, as in acute disease, a complete fast for a few days may be necessary for the elimination of toxins. Fruit juice may, however, be taken during a fast. A simple rule is : do not eat when you are sick, stick to a light diet of fresh fruits. Wait for the return of the usual healthy appetite. Loss of appetite is Nature's warning that no burden should be placed on the digestive organs. Alkaline foods such as raw vegetables and sprouted whole grain cereals may be added after a week of a fruits-only dietAnother important factor in the cure of diseases by natural methods is to stimulate the vitality of the body. This can be achieved by using water in various ways and at varying temperatures in the form of packs or baths. The application of cold water, especially to the abdomen, the seat of most diseases, and to the sexual organs, through a cold sitting (hip) bath immediately lowers body heat and stimulates the nervous system. In the form of wet packs, hydrotherapy offers a simple natural method of abating fevers and reducing pain and inflammation without any harmful side-effects.

Warm water applications, on the other hand, are relaxing. Other natural methods useful in the cure of diseases are air and sunbaths, exercise and massage. Air and sunbaths revive dead skin and help maintain it in a normal condition. Exercise, especially yogic asanas, promotes inner health and harmony and helps eliminate all tension : physical, mental and emotional. Massage tones up the nervous system and quickens blood circulation and the metabolic process.

Thus a well-balanced diet, sufficient physical exercise, the observation of the other laws of well-being such as fresh air, plenty of sunlight, pure drinking water, scrupulous cleanliness, adequate rest and right mental attitude can ensure proper health and prevent disease.

■ ■ ■

28

WAYNE DYER

SELF-HEALING THROUGH AGELESS WISDOM

Psychologist Wayne Dyer's The Wisdom of the Ages is a collection of his writings based upon the teachings of some of the greatest spiritual thinkers of the last 25 centuries. How did he get the idea for this project? "I originally was going to call this book 60 Days to Enlightenment. Abraham Maslow–who always impressed me and who was a great teacher of mine before he passed away in 1970–always talked about highly functioning, self-actualizing people. I wrote a book dedicated to him back in the 1980's called The Sky is the Limit. I later became much more intrigued with this idea of enlightenment and higher consciousness and higher awareness, and I began to look at some of the themes that are in this concept of enlightenment. Themes like agelessness, and balance, and imagination, and independence, and power, knowing and leadership, patience and inspiration. . .these kinds of ideas…and I just kept a file on them. Then I thought, if somebody could read an essay based upon these enduring kinds of lines or quotes, it would really make a nice collection. I was going to call it 60 Days to Enlightenment–the idea being here are the 60 themes, here are what people who lived at this level of enlightenment are like, and here are some ideas for you, in a short essay, to go out and practise each and every day. So this is how I started writing about it. As I began the project, it sort of unfolded in a really sweet and wonderful way."

It took him 60 days to write it spending one day studying each particular master. He would get up early in the morning and start by having a look at what their lives were like, read their biographies, find information in encyclopedias and so on. Then in the afternoon he would immerse himself in all of their writings. Some of them were artists, some of them were freedom fighters, and some of them were poets and novelists, and he would immerse himyself in their work and their message. Later in the evening, he would just look at a picture of them or an engraving of some kind, a rendering (some of them were very old), and then he would just get very quiet. He would listen, and allow them to speak to him, and he would say "What would you say to the people here today who are walking among us about these ideas that you've written about?" And the writing was done with a ball point pen and a legal pad. "Everyone was telling me that I couldn't write a book in 60 days, especially with this kind of research that's involved. I remembered what Patanjali said about inspiration–how when you're inspired by some great purpose, some extraordinary project, all of your thoughts break their bonds...your mind transcends limitations and your consciousness expands in every direction. Dormant forces, faculties and talents come alive and you discover yourself to be a greater person by far than you ever dreamed yourself to be. And I was inspired. I was literally in the world of spirit. As they say: "When the student is ready, the teachers appear." Whenever I even got mildly stuck, the right person would telephone, or something would show up in the mail. It would always just be perfect."

It was similar to a marathon, and he had done that on several occasions. It's a process called surrendering, he says. Ultimately you just realize that it's not your body that's going to get you through this thing. There's something in there called a spirit. It's like looking at a great painting and you say, "What painted that painting?" What in the physical world painted it, and when you look at it, you say, "Well the brush did, and the paint." But that's not the source of the painting. The source of the painting is in the spirit of the person who holds the brush and who dips it into the paint–so actually the source is something different.

Wayne also was a teacher for many years, and his students often would say to him, "What somebody said or lived five hundred years ago, what's that got to do with me today?" He thought this book might answer that.

What is Wayne's definition of a spiritual master? He talks about mastery in one of the essays in the book. There are four pathways to mastery. The first, the lowest pathway, is what is called the pathway of Discipline. This is the time in our lives when we train our body. We think of ourselves as having to go to practice; we have to really work hard at whatever it is we want to learn, just get some discipline. The second pathway is the pathway of Wisdom, which is the application of the mind to the discipline of the body. When we send our kids off to school, most of the time we want them to get through these first two pathways. We tell them to get some discipline and use your head, and then you'll be educated. And that's true–that's basically what education is–it's a practice of getting some discipline and using your head. But it's not mastery. The third pathway is called the pathway of Unconditional Love. You have to reach a stage or place in your life where what you are doing is something that is consistent with your sense of love for it. If you're not doing that, then you're stuck at the first or second pathway.

An example is someone who's absolutely at the top of their game–when you watch Pavarotti singing, for instance, he has great discipline. Obviously he's been to practice. And he has great wisdom; he's obviously studied. But he's not the greatest tenor on the planet because he's been to practice and because he studies more than anybody else. He conveys a great sense of love for what he is doing every time he sings. You see the bliss, you see the joy. "I think you have to get to that place. But that's still not mastery; that's approaching mastery. The highest place is called Surrender. This is when you ultimately reach mastery–when you let go and let God take over. When you surrender the little mind to the Big Mind, and allow for the idea that it's not you who's doing this. You are not what you have, you are not what you do, you are not your reputation. You are the Divine, you are connected to God, and you have reconnected to your Source in such a way that it is really God working through you, or you working with God. That's ultimately what mastery is. I've been able to get there on occasion in my writing and also in my speaking, when I really just let go. I've also been there in marathons, in tennis matches and so on, when you absolutely just let go."

Patanjali said 2300 years ago that spirit, reaching that higher place within, has certain qualities or characteristics. He said that ignorance is not being ill-informed, but ignorance is false identification–identification with the lower self, with the Ego, with the false Self and with the physical world. When you move into the world of spirituality, he said, what you are doing is you are becoming more informed in the sense that you are no longer identifying as a human being having a spiritual existence, but the other way around, as a spiritual being having a human experience. It's a new sense of identification. You begin to rewrite your agreement with your reality, with who you are and what you're here for. You see yourself as connected. Wayne thinks spirituality implies more of a sense of cheerfulness. One of the ways you're getting there is when you're more blissful on a regular basis. Most of the yogis, the gurus, the great spiritual teachers that Wayne read about or knows, almost all of them are in a constant state of bliss, he says. They can find bliss in almost anything. Also, effecting great spiritual change means not making your own quotas the source of your existence. Asking the questions, "What are your needs? How may I serve?" becomes much more important than "What's in it for me?"

"In one of my books, Manifest Your Destiny, I talk about the Four Archetypes that Jung spoke about that we progress through in our life. It's very much like the four pathways to Mastery. He said the Archetype of the Athlete is first, which is identification with our bodies, and what we can do. Next is the Archetype of the Warrior, which is when you're in your adult life and you start saying what warriors say: "How much can I get? Who can I defeat? Who am I better than and how much stuff do I have?" Then you move along to the Archetype of the Statesman or Stateswoman, which is the time when we stop asking what's in it for me, and begin to say what can I do for you? Service becomes much more important than serving self. I wrote about it in the Prayer of St. Francis. Ultimately, the Archetype of the Spirit is where you begin to see your Self, where you begin to realize that this is not your home. I think it's that recognition that this body is not who I am, this personality is not who I am, this Earth is not my home...the telling question of our existence is whether or not we have a relationship to the Infinite. If you see yourself as an infinite soul, an infinite being, sort of disguised as a person in the 21st century. I remember when they asked Mother Teresa what she did everyday she said, "Every day I see Jesus Christ in all of his distressing disguises." She would tend to the people, the Untouchables, in the streets of Calcutta. I think that's a beautiful way of phrasing it; that's sort of my take on spirituality."

What is the role of meditation in spirituality? Most people think meditation is something to do to get rid of the stress of your life, something to do to make yourself less tired, to be more energizing and so on. But not Wayne: "I think Pascal's statement "All of man's trouble stems from his inability to sit quietly in a room alone" is very significant. Most people don't know how to meditate. They don't take the time, because they don't understand the value of it. In my opinion, it's the only way you can come to make conscious contact with God. God is that which is indivisible. You can't divide it. God is One. There's no place that God is not. So when you read about people like Gandhi and Maharaj, and Jesus, and people like Ramana Maharshi and Ramakrishna, Mohammed and so on, they're called non-dual beings, people who have "transcended." Like it says in the Bhagavad Gita, "they've gone beyond the duality of the physical plane," so that there's no up and down, right and wrong, beginning and end, rich and poor–there's none of that. There's just this ONE. Meditation is a way of coming to know that Oneness. Meditation is done in silence, and in silence that's the only part of you that can't be divided. Everything else is duality. You've never seen a person with a front that doesn't have a back, with an outside that doesn't have an inside. There's this duality to the physical plane; it's always there. It's only dark because there's something called light. If it was always light there'd be no such thing as dark. So the unity is in the stillness. Stillness is indivisible, and as Melville said, God's one and only voice is silence."

That's the power of meditation: it gives you an opportunity to make conscious contact with your Source and to regain the power of your Source. The power of your Source is the power to sustain and create life; it's the power to perform miracles. It's the power to live at a level of awareness that goes beyond just ordinary human consciousness or ordinary human awareness. Patanjali speaks a great deal on that, in his original Yoga Sutras. When you begin to go to that stillness and it becomes your regular way of being, you can start to heal people by being in their presence. You can start to read minds. You can even impact natural forces just with your consciousness–that's the power of meditation to Wayne.

A lot of people don't meditate regularly because their mind wanders and they get fidgety. Wayne recommends Japa meditation. His japa has a mantra. It's the repetition of the sound of the Names for the Divine. Any Name of the Divine, any mantra, will have the same effect. Usually it has the sound "AH" in it somewhere–whether it's Yahweh, or God, or Krishna, or Allah or Ra or Kali or Durga. He lists 30 of them in Manifest Your Destiny. In the New Testament it says "In the beginning was the Word, and the Word was with God, and the Word was God." So the repetition of God is a powerful mantra. You do it outwardly at first and then inwardly.

How does he deal with tension that comes up when you're in situations you can't avoid? "My oldest son, who's 25, was telling me that he takes a shower every morning, but when he comes out of the shower and he dries off, two minutes later he's sweating just as much as before he went into the shower. And he was saying to me, "I just don't understand that." And I said, "Your mind is not at rest when you're taking a shower. During the entire time that you're in the shower, you're in a rush and you're thinking 'I have to get through this, and I have to hurry up, and I have to towel off and get dressed and I got deadlines'...Then your body is reacting just as if it were still running or exercising, because the mind controls the body. It's not the other way around." So what I said to him is this: "What I recommend is that you meditate while you shower, or just get very, very quiet. Even if you only have one minute to shower, even if your deadline is such that it's very short, treat that one minute the same way. Get very, very peaceful." And he told me the next day it was the very first time that he's come out of the shower, dried off and he wasn't sweating again. Now I do this in traffic, when I'm at a red light. Try this: When you're at a red light, recognize the fact that you have to sit there for a minute or two whether you like it or not. Now you have a choice in that two minutes–you can either sit there and fret and look at your watch and stomp and be all upset while you wait for the light to change, or you can sit there for the same two minutes and you can meditate. You can get very quiet, you can close your eyes and so on. The reality hasn't changed, nothing's changed, except you process the experience in a relaxed, and peaceful and blissful way rather than in a hurried and harried and raising up the blood pressure way. You can do this at every red light you hit for the rest of your life. You can do this in every shower; you can do this with every deadline. You can choose to deal with the deadline from the perspective that the deadline is what's causing you to be stressed, or you can remind yourself that there's no such thing as stress–there are only people thinking stressful thoughts. You can process it anyway you want to–stressfully or unstressfully."

Wayne started with Erroneous Zones and just progressed up through. Someone wrote and said he thought his book Your Sacred Self is the spiritual book of the millennium. If one were looking to perform miracles and manifest it and so on Wayne suggests Manifest Your Destiny. Or if they want to understand a basic philosophy that moves away from psychology and into spirituality, he suggests You'll See It When You

Believe It. If one would like to learn how to manage one's own emotions and not be victimized by other people, if that's a problem, then he suggests Your Erroneous Zones and Pulling Your Own Strings and The Sky's the Limit. To raise kids in a way that embraces these principles he suggests What You Really Want For Your Children.

He is now working on a book tentatively called There's a Spiritual Solution to Every Problem. "I really believe that's true in any area of our lives, so I'd really like to help define these three words: Spiritual, Solution and Problem."

■ ■ ■

Meditation

The gateway to enhance your health, mental abilities as well as emotional & spiritual well being

—Luis S.R. Vas

Meditation techniques evolved by Meditation Masters

Meditation is an ancient religious practice, being routinely prescribed in the modern secular society, not just by spiritual masters, but by behavioural scientists, medical practitioners and business consultants. It has found widely varied applications in religious institutions, medical facilities, educational establishments and business organisations. This is a relatively recent development. Less than half a century ago the word meditation, in the sense it is used today, was largely unfamiliar to those outside the Hindu and Buddhist religious traditions.

This book traces the growth of meditation around the world and focuses on several prominent meditation masters who have adapted ancient meditation practices for modern times or developed their own approaches to meditation to enhance health and mental capabilities, as well as emotional and spiritual well-being.

It concludes with a discussion on the benefits of meditation for modern men and women. The reader can try out the various techniques described and decide on the one most suited to his or her own needs.

Demy Size • Pages: 224
Price: Rs. 88/- • Postage: Rs. 15/-